The
Patriot's
Bible

ORBIS BOOKS
MARYKNOLL   NEW YORK

The Patriot's Bible

Edited by
JOHN EAGLESON
and
PHILIP SCHARPER

Acknowledgement is appreciatively extended for quotations from the following:

Richard Batey, *Jesus and the Poor* (New York: Harper & Row, 1972)

Mark J. Green et al., *The Closed Enterprise System*, Ralph Nader's Study Group Report on Antitrust Enforcement (New York: Grossman, 1972)

Woody Guthrie, "Pretty Boy Floyd," copyright 1958 by Sanga Music, Inc.

Theodore M. Hesburgh, *The Humane Imperative* (New Haven: Yale University Press, 1974)

Martin Luther King, Jr., *The Trumpet of Conscience* (New York: Harper & Row, 1967)

Martin E. Marty, *Righteous Empire: The Protestant Experience in America* (New York: Dial Press, 1970)

Gunnar Myrdal, *The Challenge of World Poverty* (New York: Vintage, 1970)

Ralph Nader and Mark J. Green, Eds., *Corporate Power in America* (New York: Grossman, 1973)

Scriptural quotations are taken from the Revised Standard Version, Catholic Edition, Old Testament copyright 1966 and New Testament copyright 1965 by Division of Christian Education of the National Council of the Churches of Christ in the United States of America.

The editors are grateful for the assistance of Anthony Larsen and David Eagleson in the preparation of *The Patriot's Bible*.

Contents

Introduction

The United States faces its third century with questions and forebodings which would have been considered almost "un-American" even ten short years ago. Recent national polls, for example, reveal that the majority of Americans have lost faith in many of our country's basic institutions.

Yet we stand neither helpless nor hopeless before the very real crises which confront us. Our basic crises are not of energy, balance of payments or the national economy. They are crises of the spirit. Our fathers brought forth on this continent a new nation—not when economic circumstances permitted it, but when their human dignity demanded it. The heritage they have bequeathed us, as well as the Judeo-Christian tradition which inspired so many of them, can provide us with sinewy spiritual resources to face challenges no greater—and no smaller—than those which they confronted.

We have attempted to draw upon both our American heritage and our broad religious tradition in compiling

The Patriot's Bible: a tapestry of passages from the Old and New Testaments, voices from the American past proclaiming our cherished first principles, statements describing both our often harsh, disheartening contemporary practices and our capacity for a change of heart, a *metanoia*.

A note about these quotations may be called for. In attempting to fashion this book, we have found that in Americophiles like Barbara Ward and Gunnar Myrdal this country often finds its true voice; on the other hand. the whole planet speaks through such different Americans as Helen Keller, Teddy Roosevelt and Theodore Hesburgh.

None of these quotations, from whatever source, have been employed as "proof texts" to establish a partisan point; but we have deliberately selected citations which emphasize the prophetic voice in both our national heritage and our religious tradition. For it is the prophet who seeks to restore a people's vision, and "where there is no vision, the people perish."

That vision is of a land which offers liberty and equal opportunity to all, a Kingdom wherein love and justice shall reign. We have tried, of course, not to confuse the Constitution with the Covenant (as many Americans have done). We further realize that our forebears did not always live out the principles they professed. The people of Israel—God's chosen people—all too often "played the harlot, forsaking their God." Some signers of the Declaration of Independence—which states that "all men are created equal"—were slaveholders. But failure to live up to noble principles does not thereby invalidate those principles.

A principled patriotism is obviously neither jingoism nor chauvinism. It is traditionally linked with devotion to one's native land, *patria*, and in our time *patria* clearly embraces this entire planet. Nothing less than a global patriotism is demanded in our third century. God so loved the *whole* world; *all* people are created equal and endowed by their Creator with certain unalienable rights. Any "more perfect union" must involve the whole human family. Our quest for "domestic tranquillity" must recognize the globe as our common domicile, our only domicile.

It is equally obvious that the principles from our past cannot be applied in mechanical fashion to the problems of our present. Frederick Douglass was confronting institutionalized slavery when he advocated struggle; St. Paul was not addressing himself to a defective welfare system when he advised the early Christians to bear each other's burdens. Yet the core values of justice and love are as valid today as they were in the eighteenth century or the first.

We must, then, creatively make our own the lofty ideals which our forebears so often captured in noble words. Those words must become flesh. Prayer and patriotism must have hands and feet. Therefore at the end of each section there are brief self-descriptions of citizens' groups attempting to incarnate those values which we have embraced as Christians and to which we commit ourselves each time we "pledge allegiance to the Flag of the United States of America and to the Republic for which it stands."

It is our hope that by offering its reader both points of reflection and guides to action *The Patriot's Bible* might serve to advance the Kingdom and further our unfinished Revolution.

John Eagleson
Philip Scharper

Some citizens of this country have never got beyond the Declaration of Independence, signed in Philadelphia, July 4th, 1776. Their bosoms swell against George III, but they have no consciousness of the war for freedom that is going on to-day.

The Declaration of Independence did not mention the questions of our day. It is of no consequence to us unless we can translate its general terms into examples of the present day and substitute them in some vital way for the examples it itself gives, so concrete, so intimately involved in the circumstances of the day in which it was conceived and written. It is an eminently practical document, meant for the use of practical men; not a thesis for philosophers, but a whip for tyrants; not a theory of government, but a program of action. Unless we can translate it into the questions of our own day, we are not worthy of it, we are not the sons of the sires who acted in response to its challenge.

What form does the contest between tyranny and freedom take to-day? What is the special form of tyranny we now fight? How does it endanger the rights of the people, and what do we mean to do in order to make our contest against it effectual? What are to be the items of our new declaration of independence?

WOODROW WILSON, twenty-eighth president of the United States, in *The New Freedom* (1913)

The only way to provide for our posterity
is to follow the counsel of the prophet Micah,
to do justly, to love mercy,
to walk humbly with our God . . . .
Beloved, there is now set before us
life and good, death and evil,
in that we are commanded this day
to love the Lord our God, and to love one another,
to walk in his ways and to keep his commandments
and his ordinance and his laws,
and the articles of our covenant with him
that we may live and be multiplied
and that the Lord our God may bless us
in the land we go to possess.
But if our hearts shall turn away
so that we will not obey
but shall be seduced and worship other Gods,
our pleasures and profits, and serve them,
it is propounded unto us this day,
we shall surely perish out of the good land
we pass over this vast sea to possess.

> *Therefore let us choose life*
> *that we and our seed may live*
> *by obeying his voice and cleaving to him,*
> *for he is our life and our prosperity* (DEUT. 30:19–20).

> > JOHN WINTHROP, first governor of Massachusetts
> > Bay Colony, in a sermon given aboard the
> > *Arbella* en route to New England (1630)

We hold these truths to be self-evident,
that all men are created equal,
that they are endowed by their Creator
with certain unalienable Rights,
that among these are Life,
Liberty,
and the pursuit of Happiness.

1

*We hold these truths
to be self-evident,
that all men
are created equal, . . .*

The Mosaic account of the creation, whether taken as divine authority, or merely historical, is fully up to this point, *the unity or equality of man*. The expressions admit of no controversy. "And God said, let us make man in our own image. In the image of God created he him; male and female created he them." The distinction of sexes is pointed out, but no other distinction is even implied. If this be not divine authority, it is at least historical authority, and shows that the equality of man, so far from being a modern doctrine, is the oldest upon record. . . .

It is one of the greatest of all truths, and of the highest advantage to cultivate. By considering man in this light, and by instructing him to consider himself in this light, it places him in a close connection with all his duties, whether to his creator, or to the creation of which he is a part; and it is only when he forgets his origin or, to use a more fashionable phrase, his *birth and family*, that he becomes dissolute.

> THOMAS PAINE, political leader in the American revolution, in *The Rights of Man* (1791)

And Peter opened his mouth and said:
"Truly I perceive that God shows no partiality,
but in every nation any one who fears him
and does what is right is acceptable to him."

ACTS 10:34–35

Looked at in his relations to God and the eternal world, every man is so valuable that you cannot make distinction between one and another.

> HENRY WARD BEECHER, clergyman, editor, and abolitionist leader, in a sermon at Plymouth Congregational Church, Brooklyn, New York (April 1862)

Let us take, for a moment, George Washington as a statesman. What was it he did, during those days when they were framing a Constitution, when they were meeting together night after night, and trying to adjust the rights and privileges of every class in the community? What was it that sustained him during all those days, all those weeks, during all those months and years? It was the belief that they were founding a nation on the axiom that all men are created free and equal. What would George Washington say if he found that among us there were causes constantly operating against that equality? If he knew that . . . every insanitary street, and every insanitary house, cripples a man so that he has no health and no vigor with which to carry on his life labor; if he knew that all about us are forces making against skill, making against the best manhood and womanhood, what would he say? He would say that if the spirit of equality means anything, it means like opportunity, and if we once lose like opportunity we lose the only chance we have toward equality throughout the nation.

> JANE ADDAMS, founder of Hull House, in her Washington's Birthday Address to the Union League, Chicago (February 1903)

This nation . . . was founded on the principle that all men are created equal, and that the rights of every man are diminished when the rights of one man are threatened . . . .

The Negro baby born in America today, regardless of the section or the state in which he is born, has about one-half as much chance of completing high school as a white baby, born in the same place, on the same day; one-third as much chance of completing college; one-third as much chance of becoming a professional man; twice as much chance of becoming unemployed; about one-seventh as much chance of earning $10,000 a year; a life expectancy which is seven years shorter and the prospects of earning only half as much . . . .

We are confronted primarily with a moral issue. It is as old as the Scriptures and is as clear as the American Constitution. The heart of the question is whether all Americans are to be afforded equal rights and equal opportunities.

> JOHN F. KENNEDY, thirty-fifth president of the United States, in a radio and television address (June 1963)

When he had washed their feet,
and taken his garments,
and resumed his place, he said to them,
"Do you know what I have done to you?
You call me Teacher and Lord;
and you are right, for so I am.
If I then, your Lord and Teacher,
have washed your feet,
you also ought to wash one another's feet.
For I have given you an example,
that you also should do as I have done to you.
Truly, truly, I say to you,
a servant is not greater than his master;
nor is he who is sent
greater than he who sent him.
If you know these things,
blessed are you if you do them."

JOHN 13:12–17

The apocalyptic thrust of Jesus' message is seen in his teaching that the kingdom would be accompanied by a reversal of the existing social order. The respected in society would reject and in turn be excluded from the kingdom, while the poor and sinners would be admitted into membership. The apocalyptic theology of reversal carried with it the understanding that the economic structure would be subjected to reform, to be brought about by God's power. The ministry of Jesus itself was a sign of this turning of the tables, when the poor would be privileged and the rich excluded.

RICHARD BATEY, Associate Professor of Bible and Religion at Southwestern at Memphis, in *Jesus and the Poor* (1972), p. 18

There you will weep and gnash your teeth,
when you see Abraham and Isaac and Jacob
and all the prophets in the kingdom of God
and you yourselves thrust out.
And men will come from east and west,
and from north and south,
and sit at table in the kingdom of God.
And behold, some are last who will be first,
and some are first who will be last.

LUKE 13:28–30

. . . all men are created equal . . .

Let us discard all this quibbling about this man and the other man—this race and that race and the other race being inferior, and therefore they must be placed in an inferior position—discarding our standard that we have left us. Let us discard all these things, and unite as one people throughout this land, until we shall once more stand up declaring that all men are created equal . . . . I leave you, hoping that the lamp of liberty will burn in your bosoms until there shall no longer be a doubt that all men are created free and equal.

> ABRAHAM LINCOLN, sixteenth president of the United States, in a campaign speech for the Senate (July 1858)

69% of *all* poor, by governmental figures, are white. . . . But

    10% of all whites are poor
    9% of all white, non-Spanish speaking are poor
    33.9% of all Blacks are poor
    24.3% of all Spanish speaking are poor
    40-50% of all Native Americans are poor.

> *Poverty Profile*, Campaign for Human Development, United States Catholic Conference (1972)

Our Constitution is colorblind and neither knows nor tolerates classes among citizens.

> JOHN MARSHALL HARLAN, Associate Justice of the U.S. Supreme Court, in sole dissent, Plessy v. Ferguson, 163 U.S. 537 (1896)

The melting pot failed to function in one crucial area. Religions and nationalities, however different, generally learned to live together, even to grow together, in

America. But color was something else. Reds were
murdered like wild animals. Yellows were charac-
terized as a peril and incarcerated en masse during
World War II for no really good reason by our most
liberal President. Browns have been abused as the new
slave labor on farms. The blacks, who did not come
here willingly, are now, more than a century after their
emancipation by Lincoln, still suffering a host of
slavelike inequalities.

> THEODORE M. HESBURGH, President of the
> University of Notre Dame, in *The New York
> Times Magazine* (October 29, 1972)

They (the founders) proclaimed to all the world the
revolutionary doctrine of the divine rights of the common man. That doctrine has ever since been the heart
of the American faith.

> DWIGHT D. EISENHOWER, thirty-fourth presi-
> dent of the United States, in his Columbia Uni-
> versity Bicentennial Address (May 1954)

The average income of Indians and Alaska Natives is
among the lowest in the United States, averaging less
than $2,000 annually per family. They are among the
most impoverished and isolated of any U. S. peoples,
and often are deprived of the basic life-serving

necessities such as good nutrition and a sanitary environment.

> *The Indian Health Program*, publication of the
> U.S. Public Health Service (August 1972)

My brethren, show no partiality
as you hold the faith of our Lord Jesus Christ,
the Lord of glory.
For if a man with gold rings and in fine clothing
comes into your assembly,
and a poor man in shabby clothing also comes in,
and you pay attention to the one
who wears the fine clothing
and say, "Have a seat here, please,"
while you say to the poor man,
"Stand there," or, "Sit at my feet,"
have you not made distinctions among yourselves,
and become judges with evil thoughts?
Listen, my beloved brethren.
Has not God chosen those who are poor in the world
to be rich in faith and heirs of the kingdom
which he has promised to those who love him?
But you have dishonored the poor man.
Is it not the rich who oppress you,
is it not they who blaspheme that honorable name
by which you are called?

JAMES 2:1–7

Our people are ebbing away like a rapidly receding tide that will never return. The white man's God cannot love our people or He would protect them. They seem to be orphans who can look nowhere for help. How then can we be brothers? How can your God become our God and renew our prosperity and awaken in us dreams of returning greatness? If we have a common Heavenly Father He must be partial—for He came to his paleface children. We never saw Him. He gave you laws but had no words for His red children whose teeming multitudes once filled this vast continent as stars fill the firmament. No. We are two distinct races with separate origins and separate destinies. There is little in common between us.

> SEALTH (SEATTLE), Chief of the Duwamish, in an address to Isaac Stevens, Governor of Washington Territory (1855)

Just because you're poor, the rich think you aren't worth anything and despise you. Suppose I live near a rich woman. And suppose her little girls want to play with mine. That rich woman would come and shoo off my children because she doesn't want hers to be friends with mine. Who the hell does she think she is? It's not right, because we're all children of God and each life is a world of its own. That's God's divine truth. But when have you seen a rich person get together with a poor one? When? That only happens in fairy tales where a princess marries a shepherd. That was in the olden times . . . . The rich want to be even richer, and instead of helping the poor, they would like to see us lower still.

> SOLEDAD, Puerto Rican slum dweller in New York, in *La Vida* by Oscar Lewis (1965), p. 148

Fourscore and seven years ago our fathers brought forth, on this continent, a new nation, conceived in Liberty, and dedicated to the proposition that all men are created equal.

> ABRAHAM LINCOLN, in his Gettysburg Address (November 1863)

I have a dream that one day this nation will rise up and live out the true meaning of its creed: "We hold these truths to be self-evident; that all men are created equal."

I have a dream that one day on the red hills of Georgia the sons of former slaves and the sons of former slaveowners will be able to sit down together at the table of brotherhood.

I have a dream that one day even the state of Mississippi, a state sweltering with the heat of injustice, sweltering with the heat of oppression, will be transformed into an oasis of freedom and justice.

I have a dream that my four little children will one day live in a nation where they will not be judged by the color of their skin but by the content of their character.

I have a dream today.

> MARTIN LUTHER KING, JR., Baptist minister, civil rights leader, Nobel Prize winner, in a speech at the Lincoln Memorial, Washington, D.C. (August 1963)

. . . all men are created equal . . .

Federal subsidies for mortgage payments are perpetuating residential segregation. In some States federally financed services to farmers still are provided on a racially discriminatory basis. Health and social services are often inaccessible to minority groups, in many instances because no provision is made for communication with persons who speak little English. Too often highways and other public works are built without considering their effect upon minority communities. In many instances, recreational facilities continue to be segregated.

> *To Know or Not to Know*, A Report of the United States Commission on Civil Rights (February 1973)

In the Lord woman is not independent of man
nor man of woman;
for as woman was made from man,
so man is now born of woman.
And all things are from God.

I CORINTHIANS II:II—I2

We hold these truths to be self-evident: that all men and women are created equal . . . . Because women do feel themselves aggrieved, oppressed, and fraudulently deprived of their most sacred rights, we insist that they have immediate admission to all the rights and privileges which belong to them.

The Seneca Falls Declaration of Sentiments (1848)

Despite women's lib and its new sister venture, corporate lib, the income gap between men and women actually widened in the '60s. In 1955, the Labor Department reports, women working full time earned 64 per cent of a man's salary; in 1970, only 59 per cent. Such statistics can be deceiving, because women tend to be less educated, to work fewer hours, and to hold a greater share of low-skilled, low-paying jobs. But even when such variables are adjusted, the most optimistic comparison shows women still earn 20 per cent less than men.

The National Observer (May 19, 1973)

Look at the Pentagon. Women are almost 41 per cent of the Defense Department. Yet, out of the 885 career and appointive employes in the top three grade levels, only five are women. Over 80 per cent of the employes in the three lowest grades are women. Our Defense Department seems more scared of giving a break to women than of giving it to the Russians.

> CLARE BOOTH LUCE, U.S. Congresswoman and Ambassador to Italy, in *U.S. News & World Report* (June 24, 1974), p. 55

When a great truth once gets abroad in the world, no power on earth can imprison it, or prescribe its limits, or suppress it. It is bound to go on till it becomes the thought of the world. Such a truth is woman's right to equal liberty with man. She was born with it. It was hers before she comprehended it. It is prescribed upon all the powers and faculties of her soul, and no custom, law nor usage can ever destroy it.

> FREDERICK DOUGLASS, black abolitionist, in a speech before the International Council of Women, Washington, D.C. (March 1888)

There is neither male nor female;
for you are all one in Christ Jesus.

GALATIANS 3:28

In effect, our world today is in reality two worlds, one rich, one poor; one literate, one largely illiterate; one industrial and urban, one agrarian and rural; one over-fed and overweight, one hungry and malnourished; one affluent and consumption-oriented, one poverty-stricken and survival-oriented. North of this line, life expectancy at birth closely approaches the biblical threescore and ten; South of it, many do not survive infancy. In the North, economic opportunities are plentiful and social mobility is high. In the South, economic opportunities are scarce and societies are rigidly stratified.

LESTER R. BROWN, Senior Fellow with the Overseas Development Council, in *World Without Borders* (1972), p. 41

. . . all men are created equal . . .

Thus says the Lord:
For three transgressions of Israel, and for four,
I will not revoke the punishment;
because they sell the righteous for silver,
and the needy for a pair of shoes—
they that trample the head of the poor
into the dust of the earth.

AMOS 2:6–7

For he delivers the needy when he calls,
the poor and him who has no helper.
He has pity on the weak and the needy,
and saves the lives of the needy.
From oppression and violence he redeems their life;
and precious is their blood in his sight.

PSALM 72:12–14

. . . with liberty and justice for all.
Pledge to the Flag

"Liberty and Justice for All" is the special theme and focus for a major program of the Catholic Church in the United States commemorating our nation's 200th anniversary. The Church's 1976 observance is being designed to increase each citizen's awareness of the need to work more strenuously for freedom and equality in today's United States.

In a like vein, the Governing Board of the National Council of Churches has called upon its constituents and all people of good will "to give thoughtful study to the beginnings of this nation, to the travail of the American Revolution and its implications for today, to the hopes and dreams of the founders and of those who have come after them, to the tragic faults and failures by which we have fallen short of our ideals, and to the ways in which those aspirations can be more fully realized in the future than they have been in the past."

The struggle for equality is never-ending. Various groups have organized to achieve the equal rights long denied them. The NATIVE AMERICAN RIGHTS FUND tries to provide Indians with their legal rights according to existing laws and treaties. These include the right to live in self-governing tribal communities, to worship according to their own beliefs, and to have their land protected in the same way as that of non-Indian farmers and homeowners. The organization aims to give Indians the same expert legal assistance as is hired by those who want to deprive them of rights and property for their own business or personal interest. For more information write NATIVE AMERICAN RIGHTS FUND, 1506 Broadway, Boulder, Colorado 80302.

Organizations committed to the interests of American Indians and run by American Indians include the AMERICAN INDIAN MOVEMENT (AIM), 704 University Avenue W., St. Paul, Minnesota 55104, and the NATIONAL CONGRESS OF AMERICAN INDIANS (NCAI), 1430 K Street, N.W., Suite 700, Washington, D.C. 20005.

The NATIONAL ORGANIZATION FOR WOMEN (NOW) is a group of women and men attempting to establish equal rights for women. They work to get employers and enforcement agencies to eradicate sex discrimination. They support precedent-setting court cases granting women equal rights. They maintain a Legislative Office in Washington and a Public Information Office in New York. Their Task Forces deal with every issue of the women's movement including credit, employment, rape, and sports. To find the local chapter nearest you, write NATIONAL ORGANIZATION FOR WOMEN, 5 South Wabash Avenue, Chicago, Illinois 60603.

THE GRAY PANTHERS are a coast-to-coast network of people ranging from sixteen to ninety-five who are determined to conquer the causes of discrimination against anyone on the basis of age. They keep tabs on medical societies, educational institutions, Congress, banks, nursing homes, employers—and any hearing aid dealer who dupes an old person into an over-priced unit that self-destructs a week later. They send out newsletters and volunteer speakers (in twos: one old Panther and one young Panther). Their address is THE GRAY PANTHERS, National Headquarters, 3700 Chestnut Street, Philadelphia, Pennsylvania 19104.

2

*. . . that they are endowed
by their Creator
with certain unalienable Rights,
that among these are Life, . . .*

The essentials for life are water and bread
and clothing and a house to cover one's nakedness.

SIRACH 29:21–22

We know that we have passed out of death into life,
because we love the brethren.
He who does not love remains in death . . . .
But if any one has the world's goods
and sees his brother in need,
yet closes his heart against him,
how does God's love abide in him?
Little children, let us not love in word or speech
but in deed and in truth.

I JOHN 3:14, 17–18

It is not charity but a right—not bounty but justice, that I am pleading for. The present state of what is called civilization is the reverse of what it ought to be. The contrast of affluence and wretchedness continually meeting and offending the eye is like dead and living bodies chained together.

THOMAS PAINE, in *Agrarian Justice* (1797)

Our cities are the abiding places of wealth and luxury; our manufactories yield fortunes never dreamed of by the fathers of the Republic; our business men are madly striving in the race for riches, and immense aggregations of capital outrun the imagination in the magnitude of their undertakings . . . . Upon more careful inspection we find the wealth and luxury of our cities mingled with poverty and wretchedness and unremunerative toil.

> GROVER CLEVELAND, twenty-second and twenty-fourth president of the United States, in his Annual Message to Congress (1888)

Here is the challenge to our democracy: In this nation I see tens of millions of its citizens—a substantial part of its whole population—who at this very moment are denied the greater part of what the very lowest standards of today call the necessities of life.

I see millions of families trying to live on incomes so meager that the pall of family disaster hangs over them day by day.

I see millions whose daily lives in city and on farm continue under conditions labeled indecent by a so-called polite society half a century ago.

I see millions denied education, recreation, and the opportunity to better their lot and the lot of their children.

I see millions lacking the means to buy the products of farm and factory and by their poverty denying work and productiveness to many other millions.

I see one-third of a nation ill-housed, ill-clad, ill-nourished.

It is not in despair that I paint you that picture. I paint it for you in hope—because the Nation, seeing and understanding the injustice in it, proposes to paint it out. We are determined to make every American citizen the subject of his country's interest and concern; and we will never regard any faithful law-abiding group within our borders as superfluous. The test of our progress is not whether we add more to the abundance of those who have much; it is whether we provide enough for those who have too little.

> FRANKLIN D. ROOSEVELT, thirty-second president of the United States, in his Second Inaugural Address (January 1937)

. . . among these are Life . . .

Poverty in the midst of plenty is a paradox that must not go unchallenged in this country. Ours is the wealthiest of nations, yet one-sixth of our people live below minimal levels of health, housing, food and education—in the slums of cities, in migratory labor camps, in economically depressed areas, on Indian reservations. In addition, special hardships are faced by our senior citizens, dependent children, and the

victims of mental illness, mental retardation and other
disabling misfortunes.

> JOHN F. KENNEDY, in a letter to Lyndon B.
> Johnson (April 1963)

President Ford has proposed new spending cuts of $4.6
billion . . . .

The proposed cuts include a $1.7 billion reduction in
medical and welfare programs administered by the
Department of Health, Education and Welfare; $1.1
billion in the Veterans Administration budget; $325
million in the food stamp program administered by the
Agriculture Department; $381 million in Defense De-
partment spending and other cuts.

The cuts would mean poor people would have to pay
more for food stamps and the elderly pay more of their
medical bills.

> Associated Press (November 27, 1974)

In a recent Gallup poll the American people selected
$6604.00/year for a family of four as a necessary in-
come to live a minimally decent life in America. The
Bureau of Labor Statistics chooses $6960.00/year as the
low-income level, enough to insure minimum food,
clothing, housing, medical care, education, transporta-
tion, insurance, plus luxuries like an occasional movie,
dessert, concert. If this last level were chosen as a

standard indicative of the real cost of living, then between *70 and 80 million people are poor.*

> *Poverty Profile,* Campaign for Human Develop-
> ment, United States Catholic Conference (1972)

*The essentials for life are water and bread
and clothing and a house to cover one's nakedness.*

> SIRACH 29:21–22

If the whole Indian subcontinent with what will soon
be a population of one billion people should sink into
the ocean tomorrow, this would cause only minor dis-
turbances to the curves of international trade, production and consumption, wages and other incomes, values of financial stocks, etc., in the developed countries.

It would hardly be noticeable in their national
economies. The developed countries need so little of
what is produced in Pakistan and India, while these
countries need so much from them.

Like many other problems in underdeveloped countries, this one also has a close parallel in the poverty
problem in the United States. There is certainly a lot of
petty cheating of the slum dwellers—by charging ex-
orbitant rents and other prices and underpaying labor
in sweatshop trades, etc. And there is plain discrimination, particularly against Negroes.

But the basic difficulty for America's large under-class in its rural and urban slums is that they have not been given the education and the skills and other personality traits they need in order to become effectively in demand in the modern economy. The parallel is even closer: there is a trend working to decrease the effective demand for the work of that underclass, making them, in fact, more and more superfluous.

If in the United States the unemployed and under-employed slum inhabitants could vanish, yes, even if all inhabitants of the slums were to vanish, there would be transitional adjustments to make but no major affliction to the national economy. After these adjustments, majority America would be as well off as before —indeed, better off, as it would have gotten rid of the large running costs for living with its slums and slum dwellers. This is the horrible truth, even if the ordinary American is not prepared to face it.

> GUNNAR MYRDAL, economist, Nobel Prize winner, in *The Challenge of World Poverty* (1970), pp. 406–07

We must be willing to abridge ourselves of our super-fluities for the supply of others' necessities.

> JOHN WINTHROP, first governor of Massachusetts Bay Colony, in a sermon aboard the *Arbella* (1630)

Mrs. Thelma Islar, a 33-year-old mother, and her four children were among the last few occupants in a battered four-story, 23-family apartment building abandoned in the Ocean Hill-Brownsville section of Brooklyn.

"We haven't had heat and hot water for a year and I have to keep the stove on all the time," she said in her kitchen on a recent frigid day, just before the city declared the structure unfit for further habitation and ordered the last four families to leave it.

All four burners on the stove were blazing, providing the only relief from the chill, and the walls were blackened from fumes caused by the stove's constant use, Mrs. Islar said.

"There are no lights in the hall and at night I have to come in and out with a flashlight," continued the woman, who is separated from her husband and is on welfare. "The building is wide open and strange people are always walking around—last night I stayed up half the night because I heard voices in the hall and I was afraid they'd break in. Five or six dogs live in the empty apartment over me. One died last summer and just dried up."

In the scarred and dank halls outside her door, fallen plaster crunched underfoot. Other apartment doors were tinned up. A row of mailboxes was ripped from the wall. A scruffy dog sniffed amid strewn garbage.

The New York Times (February 20, 1974)

*The essentials for life are water and bread
and clothing and a house to cover one's nakedness.*

SIRACH 29:21–22

About half of the nation's poor live in rural areas, often
in housing that is dilapidated and without heat or
water, but because they are scattered and without a
forceful lobby, those in the nation's countryside receive only 14 per cent of Federal housing aid. A Senate
subcommittee held hearings last week to try to find
ways to remedy that imbalance.

Rural housing inadequacies most seriously affect
blacks in the deep South, Indians, migrant farm-
workers, the aged and the black and white poor of
Appalachia, according to testimony at the hearings.

Some of the most telling testimony concerned migrant farm workers. About 18 per cent of their housing
has no electricity, 90 per cent is without sinks and 95
per cent have no flush toilets and lack tubs or showers.

The most commonly heard solutions during the
hearings were proposals to expand the Federal Farm
Home Administration and authorize it to seek increased Federal Aid for nonmetropolitan housing
needs.

That agency and the Department of Housing and
Urban Development, another agency that could help,
informed the hearings that they cannot do so because of

the anti-inflationary freeze on the release of Federal
housing aid.

The New York Times (November 24, 1974)

And who are those who suffer? Not the rich, for they
can generally take care of themselves. Capital is inge-
nious and farsighted, ready in resources and fertile in
expedients to shelter itself from impending storms.
Shut it out from one source of increase, and it will find
other avenues of profitable investment. It is the industrious, working part of the community, men whose
hands have grown hard by holding the plough and
pulling the oar, men who depend on their daily labor
and their daily pay, who, when the operations of trade
and commerce are checked and palsied, have no pros-
pect for themselves and their families but beggary and
starvation,—it is these who suffer. All this has been
attributed to causes as different as can be imagined;
over-trading, over-buying, over-selling, over-
speculating, over-production, terms which I acknowledge I do not very well understand. I am at a loss to
conceive how a nation can become poor by over-
production, producing more than she can sell or
consume.

DANIEL WEBSTER, U.S. Senator from Massachusetts, diplomat, in a speech at Madison,
Indiana (June 1837)

The needy in this country are hungrier and poorer than they were four years ago, despite great increases in spending on food programs, and rising world agricultural output has brought little benefit to the hungry abroad, a wide range of experts told the Senate today.

Furthermore, the outlook for improvement is grim without massive changes in production and distribution systems, population patterns, income levels and aid programs, the experts told the Senate Committee on Nutrition and Human Needs.

The New York Times (June 20, 1974)

At every stage, and under all circumstances, the essence of the struggle is to equalize opportunity, destroy privilege, and give to the life and citizenship of every individual the highest possible value both to himself and to the commonwealth.

THEODORE ROOSEVELT, twenty-sixth president of the United States, in a speech at Osawatomie, Kansas (August 1910)

What does it profit, my brethren,
if a man says he has faith but has not works?
Can his faith save him?
If a brother or sister is ill-clad and in lack of daily food,
and one of you says to them,

"Go in peace, be warmed and filled,"
without giving them the things needed for the body,
what does it profit?
So faith by itself, if it has no works, is dead. . . .
For as the body apart from the spirit is dead,
so faith apart from works is dead.

JAMES 2:14–17, 26

The Jewish heritage provides the background against which Jesus and his followers must be understood. The historic memory of their slavery in Egypt gave the Jewish people a special concern for the poor and oppressed. This humanitarian interest gained theological support by the faith that Yahweh in his mercy had liberated them from bondage and called them to be a people for his own possession. Therefore Yahweh's merciful character should be reflected within the society. The exploitation of a brother and even a foreigner was inexcusable. In the name of Yahweh the prophets called for social justice and obedience to the covenant laws that sought to protect the weak. It is on this tradition that Jesus drew for his teachings concerning social justice. And it is the concept of the church as the true Israel and family of God that offered the first Christians a basis for their ministry to the poor.

RICHARD BATEY, in *Jesus and the Poor* (1972), p. 97

To those peoples in the huts and villages across the globe struggling to break the bonds of mass misery, we pledge our best efforts to help them help themselves, for whatever period is required—not because the Communists may be doing it, not because we seek their votes, but because it is right. If a free society cannot help the many who are poor, it cannot save the few who are rich.

> JOHN F. KENNEDY, in his Inaugural Address (January 1961)

Incline thy ear, O Lord,
and answer me,
for I am poor and needy.

> PSALM 86:1

. . . among these are Life . . .

Our policy is directed not against any country or doctrine but against hunger, poverty, desperation, and chaos.

> GEORGE C. MARSHALL, General of the Army, Secretary of State, in an address at Harvard University (June 1947)

Agriculture Secretary Earl L. Butz said repeatedly at the World Food Conference that food is a "tool in the kit of American diplomacy," underscoring the belief of the Ford administration, like that of earlier ones, that the top priority in food aid should be to further foreign policy objectives. Food was in fact used as a weapon in the Vietnam war.

The New York Times (November 17, 1974)

Each of us living in America consumes nearly a ton of cereal grains, the best basic food and form of protein, each year. But only about 150 pounds of this is consumed directly in the form of bread, pastry, or breakfast cereals. The remaining 1,850 pounds is consumed indirectly in the form of meats, and then milk and eggs. By contrast, an average person living in a poor country has only about 400 pounds of cereal grains to consume each year for his protein. This he must take directly in the form of grains, such as rice and wheat, for little or none can be spared for conversion into more costly and inefficient means of protein production such as meat.

An acre of land can produce varying amounts of protein, depending upon how it is utilized. If you plant soybeans, you will have a yield of about 667 pounds of protein. Corn will produce 435 pounds; rice yields about 323 pounds of protein; wheat gives forth about 227 pounds. But if you devote that land to feed for poultry and meat, look what happens. For chickens, an acre will give you about 97 pounds of protein. For raising pigs, one acre of land and its feed converts into 29 pounds of protein. Finally, for every acre of land in America devoted to raising beef, we yield a mere 9 pounds of protein . . . .

The amount of food and protein consumed by the diets of 210,000,000 Americans could feed 1.5 billion Africans and Indians on a stable, though vastly different, diet.

MARK O. HATFIELD, U.S. Senator from Oregon, in *Worldview* (October 1974), p. 51

"*A man was going down from Jerusalem to Jericho,
and he fell among robbers,
who stripped him and beat him,
and departed, leaving him half-dead.
Now by chance a priest was going down that road;
and when he saw him he passed by on the other side.
So likewise a Levite,
when he came to the place and saw him,
passed by on the other side.
But a Samaritan, as he journeyed, came to where he was;
and when he saw him, he had compassion,
and went to him and bound up his wounds,
pouring on oil and wine;
then he set him on his own beast
and brought him to an inn, and took care of him.
And the next day he took out two denarii*

and gave them to the innkeeper, saying,
'Take care of him; and whatever more you spend,
I will repay you when I come back.'
Which of these three, do you think,
proved neighbor to the man who fell among the robbers?"
He said, "The one who showed mercy on him."
And Jesus said to him, "Go and do likewise."

LUKE 10:30–37

While world fertilizer supplies are inadequate because of a lack of petroleum, from which nitrogen fertilizer is made, and of a manufacturing capacity too small to meet the demand, some observers have noted that it would be possible to gather more than enough to meet India's needs by limiting the use of fertilizer for purely ornamental purposes. More fertilizer is put on American lawns, golf courses and cemeteries than India uses for food.

The New York Times (November 5, 1974)

"I was hungry and you gave me food."

MATTHEW 25:35

The consequence of prolonged hunger is malnutrition. It is widespread in the underdeveloped world. It appears to be getting worse. It hits children hardest, killing many and stunting the growth of many others both mentally and physically so that they are likely to be handicapped for life . . . .

There are no good global figures on malnutrition and never have been, but some experts estimate that a billion or more people suffer from it during at least part of the year. That means that almost a third of the human race are suffering today from hunger and its consequences . . . .

It has been estimated that roughly 15 million children a year die before the age of 5 of the combined effects of infection and malnutrition. This annual toll represents a quarter of all the deaths in the world.

The New York Times (October 6, 1974)

She lives in a tiny, three-walled mud hut in a refugee camp on the outskirts of Dacca [Bangladesh]. Every morning, dressed only in a tattered rag wound round her waist, she picks her way through the mud and filth of the camp and arrives at the office of the camp chairman. There she requests food for her three children.

And every morning the camp chairman refuses her request.

"I have no rations to give," says the chairman. "Of course," he adds, "she no longer has any children to feed. She had three children but they died last year because they had no food. Since then she is insane."

The Wall Street Journal (November 27, 1974)

Give of your bread to the hungry,
and of your clothing to the naked.
Give all your surplus to charity.

TOBIT 4:16

The earth is given as a common stock for man to labour
and live on.

THOMAS JEFFERSON, in a letter to James Madison
(1785)

The commonwealth of the future is growing surely out
of the state in which we now live . . . . Each hand will
do its part in the provision of food, clothing, shelter,
and the other great needs of man, so that if poverty
comes all will bear it alike, and if prosperity shines all
will rejoice in its warmth.

HELEN KELLER, author and lecturer, in "The
Hand of the World" (1912)

Little children, let us not love in word or speech
but in deed and in truth.

I JOHN 3:18

. . . with liberty and justice for all.
Pledge to the Flag

BREAD FOR THE WORLD is a Christian citizens' movement in the U.S.A. that is building local branches of committed members across the nation. The organization works to inform the leadership and members of the widest possible spread of Protestant, Roman Catholic, and Eastern Orthodox churches about the facts of hunger, malnutrition, and starvation among the poor both at home and abroad. They believe that most American Christians will want to do something when they know how hungry most people in the world are now and when they realize that, unless there are drastic changes, increased population and inflation will make world starvation widespread in the next decade.

Unless Congress acts wisely and generously, it will not be long before Americans will be deciding who is to live and who to starve. Members of BREAD FOR THE WORLD aim to acquaint their representatives and senators with their concern. They resist the special agricultural and business interests that too much determine United States policy. BREAD FOR THE WORLD, 602 East Ninth Street, New York, N.Y. 10009, has available a pamphlet entitled "An Alternative Diet for People Concerned About World Hunger."

The AMERICAN FREEDOM FROM HUNGER FOUNDATION seeks to arouse public awareness of the causes of hunger and malnutrition, both in the United States and abroad, and to encourage the American people to become personally involved in solving these problems. Its thrust is primarily educational, but it stresses education through personal and institutional commitment. For more information on their grass roots projects and on forming a local AFFHF committee write AMERICAN FREEDOM FROM HUNGER FOUNDATION, 110 17th Street, N.W., Suite 701, Washington, D.C. 20036.

The *Source Catalog II: Communities/Housing* describes this country's housing crisis from the perspective of what can be done by community groups. The Catalog provides a broad definition of the housing movement, covering over 700 active groups and 600 resources: books, films, and periodicals. *Source* is the most comprehensive and diverse manual for action in the housing movement to date. Brief introductions analyze each aspect of the housing system, list the basic demands of groups attacking the problems, and outline strategies for action. The Catalog is available for $2.95 from SOURCE, Box 21066, Washington, D.C. 20009.

3

. . . Liberty, . . .

Every age and generation must be as free to act for itself, *in all cases*, as the ages and generations which preceded it.

> THOMAS PAINE, in *The Rights of Man* (1791)

America is said to be the arena on which the battle of freedom is to be fought; but surely it cannot be freedom in a merely political sense that is meant. Even if we grant that the American has freed himself from a political tyrant, he is still the slave of an economical and moral tyrant.

> HENRY DAVID THOREAU, essayist and poet, in "Life Without Principle," first published posthumously in the *Atlantic Monthly* (1863)

As we view the achievements of aggregated capital, we discover the existence of trusts, combinations, and monopolies, while the citizen is struggling far in the rear or is trampled to death beneath an iron heel. Corporations, which should be the restrained creatures of the law and the servants of the people, are fast becoming the people's masters.

> GROVER CLEVELAND, in his Annual Message to Congress (1888)

. . . Liberty . . .

They promise them freedom,
but they themselves are slaves of corruption;
for whatever overcomes a man, to that he is enslaved.

                                        2 PETER 2:19

One of the chief factors in progress is the destruction of special privilege. The essence of any struggle for healthy liberty has always been, and must always be, to take from some one man or class of men the right to enjoy power, or wealth, or position, or immunity, which has not been earned by service to his or their fellows.

>   THEODORE ROOSEVELT, in a speech at Osawa-
>   tomie, Kansas (August 1910)

Thus says the Lord:
You have not obeyed me by proclaiming liberty,
every one to his brother and to his neighbor.

                                        JEREMIAH 34:17

By tyranny, as we now fight it, we mean control of the law, of legislation and adjudication, by organizations which do not represent the people, by means which are private and selfish. We mean, specifically, the conduct of our affairs and the shaping of our legislation in the interest of special bodies of capital and those who or-

ganize their use. We mean the alliance, for this purpose, of political machines with selfish business. We
mean the exploitation of the people by legal and political means. We have seen many of our governments
under these influences cease to be representative governments, cease to be governments representative of
the people, and become governments representative of
special interests, controlled by machines, which in
their turn are not controlled by the people.

> WOODROW WILSON, twenty-eighth president of
> the United States, in *The New Freedom* (1913)

Woe to those who are at ease in Zion,
and to those who feel secure
on the mountain of Samaria . . . .
O you who put far away the evil day
and bring near the seat of violence.
Woe to those who lie upon beds of ivory,
and stretch themselves upon their couches,
and eat lambs from the flock,
and calves from the midst of the stall;
who sing idle songs to the sound of the harp,
and like David invent for themselves instruments of music;
who drink wine in bowls,
and anoint themselves with the finest oils,
but are not grieved over the ruin of Joseph [Israel]!

> AMOS 6:1,3–6

Amos [the prophet] was no ascetic. His criticisms of the
rich did not rest on a belief in the evil of luxury but
rather on the violation of the covenant community.
The acquisition of wealth had been achieved by tram-
pling "the head of the poor into the dust of the earth"
(2:7, 4:1, 5:11, 8:4). Amos complained that men were
sold into slavery for failing to pay for a pair of shoes
(2:6, 8:6) or reduced to virtual nakedness by requiring
their garments as pledges against loans (2:8). Merchants enlarged their profits by false balances and inferior produce (8:5); their greed was like a canker erod-
ing their moral sensibility and social stability. The
poor could not appeal to the courts against this
economic oppression because the moneyed class controlled the decisions through the weight of their influence or bribes (2:4, 5:7, 12, 6:12). Amos saw a kind of
violence expressed through the injustices of his society
(3:10, 6:3), a violence that would not be long contained
but that would break forth and consume the nation.
This coming destruction he proclaimed was the day of
the Lord: "It is darkness and not light; as if a man fled
from a lion, and a bear met him" (5:18–19). So Amos
warned and entreated those who were in a position to
take positive action to establish justice in the gate (5:15);
"But let justice roll down like waters, and righteousness like an everflowing stream" (5:24).

> RICHARD BATEY, in *Jesus and the Poor* (1972),
> pp. 86–87

Concentration of economic power in all-embracing
corporations . . . represents private enterprise become a kind of private government which is a power
unto itself—a regimentation of other people's money
and other people's lives.

> FRANKLIN D. ROOSEVELT, in his acceptance
> speech at the Democratic National Convention
> (June 1936)

Whether the symptom is car bumpers as strong as
tissue paper, import quotas that raise the price of
gasoline by six cents a gallon, unemployment in the
steel industry when it operates at only half of its capacity, or farm subsidies that redistribute income from
working people to the rich—the problem is corporate
power. This power is not only economic—the ability
to set prices without regard to market pressures or to
manipulate consumer demand. It is also political—the
ability to use the public government to obtain private
economic goals. Corporate power means the ability of
big corporations to have more than their fair share of
influence over the decisions of government.

> FRED R. HARRIS, U.S. Senator from Oklahoma,
> in *Corporate Power in America* (1973), p. 25

By making ordinary business decisions, the managers
of firms like G.M., I.B.M., General Electric, and

Exxon now have more power than most sovereign governments to determine where people will live; what work they will do, if any; what they will eat, drink, and wear; what sorts of knowledge schools and universities will encourage; and what kind of society their children will inherit.

> RICHARD BARNET AND RONALD MÜLLER, economists, in "Global Reach," *The New Yorker* (December 2, 1974), p. 53

I am the poor white, fooled and pushed apart,
I am the Negro bearing slavery's scars,
I am the Red man driven from the land,
I am the immigrant clutching the hope I seek—
And finding only the same ole stupid plan
Of dog eat dog, of mighty crush the weak.

> LANGSTON HUGHES, black novelist and poet, in "Let America be America Again" (1938)

And I will walk among you, and will be your God,
and you shall be my people.
I am the Lord your God,
who brought you forth out of the land of Egypt,
that you should not be their slaves;
and I have broken the bars of your yoke
and made you walk erect.

> LEVITICUS 26:12–13

On July 4, 1776, Benjamin Franklin, John Adams, and Thomas Jefferson were appointed to be a "Committee to prepare a device for a Seal of the United States of America." Numerous suggestions were offered. Franklin advocated a design which featured Moses. In the background, the troops of Pharaoh would be seen drowning in the Red Sea: "Rebellion to tyrants is obedience to God." Jefferson's suggestion contained elements that were to be included in the adopted seal. The children of Israel in the wilderness were "led by a cloud by day and a pillar of fire by night." While this biblical content nearly evaporated by the time of final adoption, it is significant that these statesmen—in so many ways uneasy themselves about the Jewish-Christian heritage—drew upon the Bible for symbols which could unite and interpret their people's experience.

In the years that were to follow, Americans would again and again read themselves into the stories of the Biblical Exodus and deliverance from tyranny and slavery. For most people the acts of coming to America and becoming independent were completed acts of freedom and deliverance. For a very large minority, however, the use of such symbols was expressive of vague promise and desperate hope. They were in America, but not yet fully of it. They had not been rescued or liberated. And when these black Americans would evoke the symbols of Exodus they looked subversive to those around them. Not for one hundred years did most of them have even a minimal legal experience of liberation. They were to know many a Moses, but were to be denied a promised land.

> MARTIN E. MARTY, religious historian, in *Righteous Empire: The Protestant Experience in America* (1970), p. 24

Of all the various modes and forms of government, that is best which is capable of producing the greatest degree of happiness and safety, and is most effectually secured against the danger of maladministration; and that when any government shall be found inadequate, or contrary to those purposes, a majority of the community hath an indubitable, unalienable and indefeasible right to reform, alter or abolish it, in such manner as shall be judged most conducive to the public weal.

> *The Virginia Bill of Rights* (1776)

Remember always that all of us, and you and I especially, are descended from immigrants and revolutionists.

> FRANKLIN D. ROOSEVELT, in a speech to the Daughters of the American Revolution (April 1938)

Is not this the fast that I choose:
to loose the bonds of wickedness,
to undo the thongs of the yoke,
to let the oppressed go free,
and to break every yoke?

ISAIAH 58:6

I hold it, that a little rebellion, now and then, is a good thing, and as necessary in the political world as storms in the physical.

THOMAS JEFFERSON, in a letter to James Madison (January 1787)

They shall know that I am the Lord,
when I break the bars of their yoke,
and deliver them from the hand
of those who enslaved them.

EZEKIEL 34:27

Those who won our independence by revolution were not cowards. They did not fear political change. They did not exalt order at the cost of liberty.

LOUIS D. BRANDEIS, jurist, Associate Justice of the U.S. Supreme Court, in concurring opinion, Whitney v. California, 274 U.S. 357 (1927)

Live Free or Die.

> State Motto of New Hampshire

It is the unhappy fact that the United States in recent years has thrown its support against *all* revolutions and provided its backing for *all* groups that have opposed revolutions, regardless of the merits of the one or the demerits of the other—the scandal of our Dominican invasion, our Guatemalan "success," and our Cuban "failure," our backing of the militarist Branco in Brazil, and now our intervention in Vietnam all being instances in point. In the essential process of social surgery that must be performed if many backward nations are to be brought to life, it is the United States—for good reasons or bad—that delays the necessary stroke of the blade. That is why the revolution of economic development must become an anti-American revolution unless the United States changes its ways.

> ROBERT L. HEILBRONER, economic historian, in
> *Harper's Magazine* (September 1968), pp. 69–70

The director of the Central Intelligence Agency has told Congress that the Nixon Administration authorized more than $8-million for covert activities by the agency in Chile between 1970 and 1973 in an effort to make it impossible for President Salvador Allende Gossens to govern.

The goal of the clandestine C.I.A. activities, the director, William E. Colby, testified at a top-secret hearing last April, was to "destabilize" the Marxist Government of President Allende, who was elected in 1970.

The Allende Government was overthrown in a violent coup d'état last Sept. 11 in which the President died.

The New York Times (September 8, 1974)

Honoring the identity and the special heritage of each nation in the world, we shall never use our strength to try to impress upon another people our own cherished political and economic institutions.

DWIGHT D. EISENHOWER, in his First Inaugural Address (January 1953)

. . . Liberty . . .

Again I saw all the oppressions
that are practiced under the sun.
And behold, the tears of the oppressed,
and they had no one to comfort them!

On the side of the oppressors there was power,
and there was no one to comfort them.
And I thought the dead who are already dead
more fortunate than the living who are still alive;
but better than both is he who has not yet been,
and has not seen the evil deeds
that are done under the sun.

ECCLESIASTES 4:1–3

Visit the favelas, barriadas, villas miserias, and callam-pas surrounding the Latin American capital cities, step aboard the floating junks adjacent to Hong Kong's harbor, look at the native locations north of Johannes-burg in South Africa, or inspect some of America's own inner city slums, Chicano colonias in the South-west, or miners' rotting villages in Appalachia, or al-most any American Indian reservation in the West. It isn't just what you see that will sicken you. It is that it is all so unnecessary, that it is man-made and man-kept, and that it is in startling contrast to the way other humans are living in luxury only a few miles away from each of these human sewers and garbage heaps.

An easy answer would be to say that there are just not enough of the world's resources to house and feed everyone. But then remember that last year, and for most of the years we can remember, the governments of this planet have spent more than $200 billion on armaments—and that is more than the total annual income of the poorest half of the earth's population. We do it because the Russians do it, and they do it because we do it, and so the foolishness goes on and on and on, all around the world. Meanwhile, the poor go to bed hungry, when they are lucky enough to have beds.

> THEODORE M. HESBURGH, in *The Humane Imperative* (1974), p. 101

A hungry man is not a free man.

> ADLAI E. STEVENSON, statesman, ambassador to the United Nations, in a campaign speech (September 1952)

Proclaim Liberty throughout all the Land
to all the Inhabitants thereof.

> LEVITICUS 25:10
> *(Inscription on the Liberty Bell)*

From every mountainside, let freedom ring. And when this happens—when we let freedom ring, when we let it ring from every village and every hamlet, from every state and every city, we will be able to speed up that day when all of God's children, black men and white men, Jews and Gentiles, Protestants and Catholics, will be able to join hands and sing in the words of the old Negro spiritual, "Free at last! free at last! thank God almighty, we are free at last!"

> MARTIN LUTHER KING, JR., in a speech at the Lincoln Memorial, Washington, D.C. (August 1963)

On the limits of liberty and justice, honorable men, committed men deeply disagree. For the extension of liberty may somehow diminish justice, or an even distribution of justice may limit liberty. Neither is ever perfectly achieved; nevertheless the American credo calls for loyalty to both as long-range ideals and as short-range practical programs. In loyalty to America's creed as well as to their own, synagogues and churches could not escape the demands of liberty under justice for all.

Freedom of religion in America includes, of course, the right of religion to be inane, impotent, and toothless: to be, in short, what Marx called the opiate of the people. That freedom, however, can also be used to proclaim repentance, reform, and, if need be, even revolution. The struggle for "liberty and justice for all" is never wholly won, but only when that struggle ceases is the battle wholly lost.

> EDWIN SCOTT GAUSTAD, religious historian, in
> *A Religious History of America* (1966), p. 345

You were called to freedom, brethren.

GALATIANS 5:13

Is true Freedom but to break
Fetters for our own dear sake,
And, with leathern hearts, forget
That we owe mankind a debt?
No! True Freedom is to share
All the chains our brothers wear,
And, with heart and hand, to be
Earnest to make others free!

JAMES RUSSELL LOWELL, poet, essayist, diplomat, in "Stanzas on Freedom" (1843)

. . . with liberty and justice for all.
Pledge to the Flag

Liberty is today being denied uncounted individuals throughout the world. AMNESTY INTERNATIONAL works for the release of persons imprisoned, restricted, or detained because of their political, religious, or other conscientiously held beliefs, or by reason of their ethnic origin, color, or language, provided they have neither used nor advocated violence. The organization endeavors to aid and secure the release of these prisoners of conscience through investigation, "adoption," financial and legal assistance to them and their families, working to improve their conditions while imprisoned or detained, and publicizing their plight wherever desirable. There are several ways of contributing to the organization's work: (1) Join or form an Amnesty group, which is assigned three prisoners. The group then directs an insistent, continuous, and informed appeal to the relevant governments and prison officials urging a reconsideration of the case and the release of the prisoner. (2) Write letters concerning the prisoners listed in their monthly newsletter. (3) Send the group press clippings on prisoners and prison conditions. (4) Send a contribution and recruit new members. For more information write AMNESTY INTERNATIONAL OF THE U.S.A., 200 West 72nd Street, New York, New York 10023.

THE PEOPLE'S BICENTENNIAL COMMISSION is a nationwide citizen organization dedicated to restoring the democratic principles that shaped the birth of this republic. Believing there is more to the Spirit of '76 than plastic liberty bells and stars and stripes toothpaste, the organization calls for allegiance to the revolutionary principles that launched our first national rebellion to tyranny. The PBC provides a broad selection of literature and program materials for local groups and schools who also seek revolutionary alternatives for the Bicentennial Years. For more information write THE

PEOPLE'S BICENTENNIAL COMMISSION, 1346 Connecticut Avenue, N.W., Washington, D.C. 20036.

The AMERICAN CIVIL LIBERTIES UNION (ACLU) is a permanent, national, non-partisan organization with the single purpose of defending the whole Bill of Rights for everybody. They believe that defending the civil liberties of even the hated and feared must be undertaken in order to prevent the decay of everybody else's constitutional rights. By joining the ACLU you automatically become part of a local ACLU affiliate in your area, thereby enabling you to become part of civil liberties activities in your community. Write ACLU, 22 East 40th Street, New York, New York 10016.

4

. . . : and the pursuit of Happiness.

There is great gain in godliness with contentment;
for we brought nothing into the world,
and we cannot take anything out of the world;
but if we have food and clothing,
with these we shall be content.
But those who desire to be rich
fall into temptation, into a snare,
into many senseless and hurtful desires
that plunge men into ruin and destruction.
For the love of money
is the root of all evils;
it is through this craving
that some have wandered away from the faith
and pierced their hearts with many pangs.

1 TIMOTHY 6:6–10

Seek not to be Rich, but Happy. The one lies in Bags, the other in Content: which Wealth can never give.

We are apt to call things by wrong Names. We will have Prosperity to be Happiness, and Adversity to be Misery . . . .

If thou wouldest be Happy, bring thy Mind to thy Condition, and have an Indifferency for more than what is sufficient.

WILLIAM PENN, Quaker leader, founder of Pennsylvania, in his *Some Fruits of Solitude* (1693), nos. 238–40

When it shall be said in any country in the world, my poor are happy: neither ignorance nor distress is to be found among them; my jails are empty of prisoners, my streets of beggars; the aged are not in want, the taxes are not oppressive; the rational world is my friend, because I am the friend of its happiness: when these things can be said, then may that country boast of its constitution and its government.

THOMAS PAINE, in *The Rights of Man* (1791)

Turning our eyes to other nations, our great desire is to see our brethren of the human race secured in the blessings enjoyed by ourselves, and advancing in knowledge, in freedom, and in social happiness.

ANDREW JACKSON, seventh president of the United States, in an address to Congress (December 1829)

You hear of people paying all kinds of money for houses and condominiums these days. But even in these inflationary times, $155,000 for a one-bedroom apartment seems a trifle steep.

Of course, that's on the 49th floor. A bargain hunter can still snap up an identical apartment on the 23rd floor for only $122,000—if he doesn't mind the stigma of buying the cheapest apartment the building still has to offer. On the other hand, those who don't like to skimp can always buy a four-bedroom duplex penthouse for $620,000. It will have a private sauna and an internal elevator that travels one flight.

That's the way things are at the Olympic Tower condominium building, Fifth Avenue's latest lure for the very rich. The concierge will be trained to charter yachts on short notice. A tenant will be able to wire his Rembrandts into a computerized security system. The apartment doorways will be trimmed in antique-green marble . . . .

Other conveniences and luxuries include a health club, an international newsstand and 24-hour valet service. The building will have its own wine cellar. There will be an indoor park with its own three-story-high waterfall. And if the barbershop in the building seems too inconvenient, the barber will come to you.

The Wall Street Journal (October 21, 1974)

. . . and the pursuit of Happiness.

And as he was setting out on his journey,
a man ran up and knelt before him, and asked him,
"Good Teacher, what must I do to inherit eternal life?"
And Jesus said to him,
"Why do you call me good? No one is good but God alone.

You know the commandments:
'Do not kill, Do not commit adultery,
Do not steal, Do not bear false witness,
Do not defraud, Honor your father and mother.' "
And he said to him,
"Teacher, all these I have observed from my youth."
And Jesus looking upon him loved him, and said to him,
"You lack one thing;
go, sell what you have, and give to the poor,
and you will have treasure in heaven;
and come, follow me."
At that saying his countenance fell,
and he went away sorrowful; for he had great possessions.
And Jesus looked around and said to his disciples,
"How hard it will be for those who have riches
to enter the kingdom of God!"
And the disciples were amazed at his words.
But Jesus said to them again,
"Children, how hard it is for those who trust in riches
to enter the kingdom of God!
It is easier for a camel to go through the eye of a needle
than for a rich man to enter the kingdom of God."
And they were exceedingly astonished, and said to him,
"Then who can be saved?"
Jesus looked at them and said,
"With men it is impossible, but not with God;
for all things are possible with God."

MARK 10:17–27

To be in the kingdom meant having faith in the sovereignty of a compassionate Father and reflecting his sovereignty within the unjust social order. The obdurate acquiring and possession of wealth in the midst of human misery and suffering is evil in itself, because it is a rejection of this compassion. Jesus' admonition was not to lay up treasures on earth, but to seek first the Kingdom of God; material things would then come in their proper place (Matt. 6:33; Luke 12:31) . . . .

To the poor and common people Jesus affirmed their acceptability before God. They were not to consider their lack of health and wealth as a sign of divine disapproval, for indeed, of their numbers the ranks in the kingdom would be filled. But Jesus warned them against making the same mistake as the rich. They, too, could not consider the possession of goods as the true measure of life. He challenged them not to be preoccupied with physical needs, for which deprivation often created an obsession. Anxiety about food and clothing does not portray that basic trust in the creative power that sustains the life even of the birds of the air and the grass and lilies of the field. Such anxiety feeds on the ignorance of the source of true life and compels one to attempt to secure life by amassing wealth or collecting things (Matt. 6:25–33).

RICHARD BATEY, in *Jesus and the Poor* (1972), p. 17

Are not five sparrows sold for two pennies?
And not one of them is forgotten before God.
Why, even the hairs of your head are all numbered.
Fear not; you are of more value than many sparrows.

LUKE 12:6–7

No servant can serve two masters;
for either he will hate the one and love the other,
or he will be devoted to the one and despise the other.
You cannot serve God and mammon.

LUKE 16:13

Do not lay up for yourselves treasures on earth,
where moth and rust consume
and where thieves break in and steal,
but lay up for yourselves treasures in heaven,
where neither moth nor rust consumes
and where thieves do not break in and steal.
For where your treasure is,
there will your heart be also.

MATTHEW 6:19–21

Happiness lies not in the mere possession of money; it lies in the joy of achievement, in the thrill of creative effort. The joy and moral stimulation of work no longer must be forgotten in the mad chase of evanescent profits. These dark days will be worth all they cost us if they teach us that our true destiny is not to be ministered unto but to minister to ourselves and to our fellow men.

FRANKLIN D. ROOSEVELT, in his Inaugural Address (March 1933)

Among us English-speaking peoples especially do the praises of poverty need once more to be boldly sung. We have grown literally afraid to be poor. We despise anyone who elects to be poor in order to simplify and save his inner life. If he does not join the general scramble and pant with the money-making street, we deem him spiritless and lacking in ambition. We have lost the power even of imagining what the ancient idealization of poverty could have meant: the liberation from material attachments, the unbribed soul, the manlier indifference, the paying our way by what we are or do and not by what we have, the right to fling away our life at any moment irresponsibly—the more athletic trim, in short, the moral fighting shape. . . .

Think of the strength which personal indifference to poverty would give us if we were devoted to unpopular causes. We need no longer hold our tongues or fear to vote the revolutionary or reformatory ticket. Our stocks might fall, our hopes of promotion vanish, our salaries stop, our club doors close in our faces; yet, while we lived, we would imperturbably bear witness to the spirit, and our example would help to set free our generation. . . .

I recommend this matter to your serious pondering, for it is certain that the prevalent fear of poverty among the educated classes is the worst moral disease from which our civilization suffers.

WILLIAM JAMES, philosopher and psychologist, in *The Varieties of Religious Experience* (1902)

What a life.

It's not just what you do. It's where you do it. Do it. Down in the Caribbean. In the United States Virgin Islands.

In sunlight. Having a beach all to yourself. Yachting and swimming and skin-diving. Golfing and tennis and deep-sea fishing. Sightseeing through old plantations and hideouts of pirates. Shopping down alleyways in old Danish warehouses.

In moonlight. Rattling your diamonds in a discotheque. Biting a lobster and sipping a wine. Dancing in the cool of emerald hills. Finding a jazzy little jazzspot by the sea.

Day and night. Meeting the mix of people in the islands. It is they who keep things stylish and informal. Casual chic, so to speak.

Getting to the islands is as simple as a nonstop flight from New York City.

> Advertisement in *Time* (November 25, 1974)

. . . and the pursuit of Happiness.

And others are the ones sown among thorns;
they are those who hear the word,
but the cares of the world, and the delight in riches,
and the desire for other things,
enter in and choke the word, and it proves unfruitful.

> MARK 4:18–19

No wealth in the world can help humanity forward, even in the hands of the most devoted worker in this cause . . . . Can anyone imagine Moses, Jesus, or Gandhi armed with the money-bags of Carnegie?

> ALBERT EINSTEIN, theoretical physicist, in *Ideas and Opinions* (1954)

The General Motors Corporation disclosed today that its chairman, Richard C. Gerstenberg, received a 5.5 per cent raise last year, lifting his total compensation by $48,037 to $923,000 and keeping him well in the lead as the highest paid executive in the country.

The New York Times (April 19, 1974)

The General Motors Corporation, reflecting one of the severest declines in the automobile industry since World War II, announced today additional layoffs and production cutbacks for the first quarter of 1975.

An additional 16,000 workers will be put on permanent layoff and 41,000 will be on temporary layoffs for from one to four weeks during January. Today's announcement means that General Motors alone will have 91,000 workers laid off permanently and another 41,000 affected by temporary layoffs in January. The permanent layoffs amount to about one quarter of G.M.'s hourly work force.

The New York Times (December 19, 1974)

"If any man would come after me, let him deny himself
and take up his cross daily and follow me.
For whoever would save his life will lose it;
and whoever loses his life for my sake,
he will save it.
For what does it profit a man
if he gains the whole world and loses or forfeits himself?"

LUKE 9:23–25

On the issue of justice, Christian doctrine allows no evasion. Dives leaving Lazarus to sicken at his gate, the rich man rebuilding his barns for the selfish consumption of a larger harvest, the priest and levite "passing by on the other side"—these parables of justice and judgment meet us on every page of the Bible and the final gathering in of God's people turns on one thing only —that the hungry are fed, the naked clothed, prisoners visited, the afflicted given comfort. These are the gestures of love. But they are not left to our choice. Justice is the command to which love responds. To refuse is to "choose death."

Modern man's discovery of possible economic and natural limits to the processes of production has a further significance. Christian doctrine has never believed that "self-love and social" are the same. On the contrary, greed, avarice, rapacity and careless waste destroy men and destroy society. To suppose that the unfettered pursuit of unlimited wealth would not, in Emerson's words, "go on to madness" contradicts every beatitude pronounced by Christ. If the strong, the rich, the rapacious and the careless "inherit the earth," then there is no meaning in the Christian Gospel. But if today the pressures of material reality in the shape of possibly less abundant resources and a certainly growing deterioration in the natural environment begin to compel men and women to reconsider the goal of unlimited consumption and to stop seeking felicity in the latest car, the latest drink, the latest jet and the latest cosmetic, the Christian can say that the physical world is beginning to reaffirm the unchanging wisdom of the moral order. We do not choke or swill or waste our way to beatitude.

> BARBARA WARD, Professor of International Economic Development at Columbia University, in *A New Creation?: Reflections on the Environmental Issue* (1973), p. 59

There has been something crude and heartless and unfeeling in our haste to succeed and be great. Our thought has been "Let every man look out for himself, let every generation look out for itself," while we reared giant machinery which made it impossible that any but those who stood at the levers of control should have a chance to look out for themselves. We had not forgotten our morals. We remembered well enough that we had set up a policy which was meant to serve the humblest as well as the most powerful, with an eye single to the standards of justice and fair play, and remembered it with pride. But we were very heedless and in a hurry to be great.

We have come now to the sober second thought. The scales of heedlessness have fallen from our eyes. We have made up our minds to square every process of our national life again with the standards we so proudly set up at the beginning and have always carried at our hearts. Our work is a work of restoration.

> WOODROW WILSON, in his Inaugural Address
> (March 1913)

> **. . . with liberty and justice for all.**
> *Pledge to the Flag*

Many Americans today are acutely aware that "happiness" does not mean more money or increased consumption. ALTERNATIVES is a group created for the purpose of action/education in the area of alternative lifestyles, institutions, and social change methods. One of their projects is the *Alternate Christmas Catalogue*, which is based on the alternatives of celebrating simply, making gifts, buying from self-help craft groups, and diverting money to people-and-earth orientated projects. Their *Catalogue*, containing ideas on non-materialistic, non-consumptive approaches to "the pursuit of happiness" is available from ALTERNATIVES, 1500 Farragut St., N.W., Washington, D.C. 20011.

We the People of the United States
in Order to form a more perfect Union,
establish Justice,
insure domestic Tranquillity,
provide for the common defence,
promote the general Welfare,
and secure the Blessings of Liberty
to ourselves and our Posterity . . .

5

We the People
of the United States, . . .

Government is instituted for the common good, for the protection, safety, prosperity, and happiness of the people and not for the profit, honor, or private interest of any one man, family, or class of men.

> JOHN ADAMS, second president of the United States, in his proposed Constitution of Massachusetts (1780)

The government of the Union, then, . . . is, emphatically, and truly, a government of the people. In form and in substance it emanates from them. Its powers are granted by them, and are to be exercised directly on them, and for their benefit.

> JOHN MARSHALL, statesman, jurist, Chief Justice of the United States, in McCulloch v. Maryland, 4 Wheaton 316 (1819)

If particular care and attention is not paid to the ladies, we are determined to foment a rebellion, and will not hold ourselves bound by any laws in which we have no voice or representation.

> ABIGAIL ADAMS, writer, in a letter to her husband John (March 1776)

It was we, the people; not we, the white male citizens; nor yet we, the male citizens; but we, the whole people, who formed the Union. And we formed it, not to give the blessings of liberty, but to secure them; not to the half of ourselves and the half of our posterity, but to the whole people—women as well as men.

> SUSAN B. ANTHONY, leader in woman suffrage movement, in a speech at New York (1873)

Ironically, women's suffrage finally came first in the wide-open West, in part as a way of fighting off immigrant influences by assuring enough "Puritan" votes. As University of Colorado President (emeritus) James H. Baker said in 1927, "Puritan standards have become the public standards of America, and you will find more of New England in Colorado Springs, Boulder, or Greeley than in most towns of Massachusetts." The suffrage success came in part over against Roman Catholics, eastern political leaders, and the foreign born. The Protestants' men in their own way had won another round, temporarily—even though they had to accept ideas which only decades earlier their fathers had contended were against the Scriptural view of women.

> MARTIN E. MARTY, in *Righteous Empire: The Protestant Experience in America* (1970), p. 204

This country, with its institutions, belongs to the people who inhabit it. Whenever they shall grow weary of the existing Government, they can exercise their *constitutional* right of amending it or their *revolutionary* right to dismember or overthrow it.

> ABRAHAM LINCOLN, in his First Inaugural Address (March 1861)

We the People of the United States . . .

Its [the Constitution's] language is, "We the people"; not we the white people, not even we the citizens, not we the privileged class, not we the high, not we the low, but we the people; not we the horses, sheep, and swine, and wheelbarrows, but we the people, we the human inhabitants; and if Negroes are people, they are included in the benefits for which the Constitution of America was ordained and established.

> FREDERICK DOUGLASS, in a lecture at Rochester, New York (1885)

I swear to the Lord
I still can't see
Why Democracy means
Everybody but me.

> LANGSTON HUGHES, in "The Black Man Speaks" (1943)

You shall not oppress a stranger;
you know the heart of a stranger,
for you were strangers in the land of Egypt.

EXODUS 23:9

Give me your tired, your poor,
Your huddled masses yearning to breathe free,
The wretched refuse of your teeming shore,
Send these, the homeless, tempest-tost, to me,
I lift my lamp beside the golden door!

> EMMA LAZARUS, poet and philanthropist, in
> "The New Colossus," inscription for the Statue
> of Liberty, New York Harbor (1883)

A Puerto Rican up here has a hard time finding a job
and a safe place to live. If you're a Puerto Rican you can
apply in twenty thousand places without getting a job.
You can't get a job in a hospital or in the big department
stores. But go to the factories, the cheap, ratty ones,
and there you find Puerto Ricans, earning miserable
wages. In the best places you find only Americans,
never a Puerto Rican.

> SOLEDAD, slum dweller in New York, in *La Vida*
> by Oscar Lewis (1965), p. 211

We the People of the United States . . .

Therefore, you shepherds, hear the word of the Lord:
As I live, says the Lord God,
because my sheep have become a prey,
and my sheep have become food for all the wild beasts,
since there was no shepherd;
and because my shepherds have not searched for my sheep,
but the shepherds have fed themselves,
and have not fed my sheep. . . .
Behold, I am against the shepherds;
and I will require my sheep at their hand,
and put a stop to their feeding the sheep,
no longer shall the shepherds feed themselves.
I will rescue my sheep from their mouths,
that they may not be food for them.

EZEKIEL 34:7–10

Next in importance to the maintenance of the Constitution and the Union is the duty of preserving the Government free from the taint or even the suspicion of corruption. Public virtue is the vital spirit of republics, and history proves that when this has decayed and the love of money has usurped its place, although the forms of the free government may remain for a season, the substance has departed forever.

JAMES BUCHANAN, fifteenth president of the United States, in his Inaugural Address (March 1857)

The citizens of the United States must effectively control the mighty commercial forces which they have themselves called into being. There can be no effective control of corporations while their political activity remains. To put an end to it will be neither a short nor an easy task, but it can be done.

> THEODORE ROOSEVELT, in a speech at Osawatomie, Kansas (August 1910)

We the People of the United States . . .

The masters of the government of the United States are the combined capitalists and manufacturers of the United States. It is written over every intimate page of the records of Congress, it is written all through the history of conferences at the White House, that the suggestions of economic policy in this country have come from one source, not from many sources. . . .

Suppose you go to Washington and try to get at your government. You will always find that while you are politely listened to, the men really consulted are the men who have the biggest stake—the big bankers, the big manufacturers, the big masters of commerce, the heads of railroad corporations and of steamship corporations.

> WOODROW WILSON, in *The New Freedom* (1913)

Recently a careful study was made of the concentration of business in the United States. It showed that our economic life was dominated by some six hundred odd corporations who controlled two-thirds of American industry. Ten million small business men divided the other third. More striking still, it appeared that if the process of concentration goes on at the same rate, at the end of another century we shall have all American industry controlled by a dozen corporations, and run by perhaps a hundred men. But plainly, we are steering a steady course toward economic oligarchy, if we are not there already.

> FRANKLIN D. ROOSEVELT, in his Commonwealth Club Address (September 1932)

Corporate power in the political process is a reality. You don't have to believe that, somewhere, there are twelve bankers, politicians, and corporate executives who meet once a week to decide the future of America—there aren't—to see that General Motors has more to say about federal air pollution standards than you or I or even millions like us do. And you don't have to believe that politicians regularly receive bribes —they don't—to see that David Rockefeller gets a better hearing in Congress than does the average American workingman or woman. Why violate the law by bribing public officials when there are legal and more traditional methods of persuasion that are more

effective? Among these methods are campaign contributions, advertising, lobbying, and government-
business job exchanges.

> FRED R. HARRIS, U.S. Senator from Oklahoma,
> in *Corporate Power in America* (1973), pp. 26–27

I think basically you have to start with a realization that
the country is principally run by big business for the
rich. Maybe you have to live in Washington to know
that and maybe everyone in the country knows it intu-
itively, I don't know, but a government of the people,
by the people, and for the people has become, I think, a
government of the people, certainly, but by the corporations and for the rich.

> NICHOLAS JOHNSON, member of the Federal
> Communications Commission, quoted in
> *Monthly Review* (November 1969), p. 11

Under God the people rule.

> State Motto of South Dakota

The distribution of income in the United States has not
changed materially in a generation, through at least
four recessions, four serious inflation attacks, and
numerous allegedly major changes in the tax laws.

Nor has there been any statistically significant

change in the distribution of the country's other big pie, wealth, over the same period . . . .

How . . . can 60 percent of the people expect to get very far ahead in life, when the economy pays them less than 35 percent of each year's total family income?

Or, put another way, how much is there going to be for the vast majority of the public, if on the wealthier end of the economic scale, 20 percent of families cut up nearly half of all of the national family income every year—and even more significant, a scant 5 percent of families are dividing nearly 16 percent of that total income? . . .

These numbers concerning the distribution of income to US families are not new; in fact, they have not appreciably changed since the end of World War II, and thus constitute a powerful argument in favor of the notion that while this country may not have princes and princesses, lords and ladies, there is still a remarkably rigid economic pecking order.

The Boston Globe (May 12, 1974)

Hear the word of the Lord, O people of Israel;
for the Lord has a controversy
with the inhabitants of the land.
There is no faithfulness or kindness,
and no knowledge of God in the land.

HOSEA 4:1

Money runs the politics of your country, it has nothing to do with morality or anything else. So, all the slick-talkers in the world really can't overcome the existing situation without bags of money. Face reality; we The People, have been very aware for many moons that big business doesn't give a hoot about the people. This means you and us! Big business is interested only in big money. People are of value only so long as they pro-duce for big business. We, The Native People, are a dead-loss to big business because we, as a race, are not on their money-trip. We are further a dead-weight because of our love of the land. We have reached the point that we are fighting to preserve this land. Big business views the land as something to strip! Look at what Crown Zellerbach has done right here, where they have strip timbered the land. Look where big business has strip mined the land, ravaged the vegeta-tion, polluted rivers and reduced water tables to well below the danger point. This is big business, and un-less things change, *you* will see this land ravaged into a total desert, and all for big business. In reality, our enemy is the same as yours. WE are not enemies.

N. MAGOWAN, editor-publisher of the *Cherokee Examiner*, in *Rainbow People*, vol. 1, no. 3 (1970)

When one rules justly over men,
ruling in the fear of God,

he dawns on them like the morning light,
like the sun shining forth upon a cloudless morning,
like rain that makes grass to sprout from the earth.

2 SAMUEL 23:3–4

We the People of the United States . . .

Three out of four Americans, according to that poll [a Harris poll published June 27, 1974], believe that the tax laws are written to help the rich and not the average man; 78 percent believe that special interests get more from the government than the people do; and 79 percent (almost four out of five Americans) now believe that the rich get richer and the poor get poorer. What these figures mean, when added to similar results in other major polls, is that the postwar dream of Corporate America as an increasingly egalitarian and democratic society is over. Or, quoting the Harris survey:

> Disenchantment with the state of the country has now reached such massive proportions among the American people that a record high 59 per cent now feel disaffected, up from 55 per cent in 1973 and more than double the 29 per cent who felt that way back in 1966.

> So pervasive is the feeling that no less than a majority of every single major segment of the population

is turned off by politics, the [un]fairness of the economic system and the role accorded the individual in society.

But to be turned off by the unfairness of the system is not equivalent to understanding why the system works that way or, better yet, what can be done about it. What we are witnessing is the emergence of a radicalism or populism that is apolitical and cynical.

ROBERT SCHEER, political economist, in *America After Nixon* (1974), pp. xiv–xv

It is rather for us to be here dedicated to the great task remaining before us—that from these honored dead we take increased devotion to that cause for which they here gave the last full measure of devotion—that we here highly resolve that these dead shall not have died in vain—that this nation, under God, shall have a new birth of freedom—and that government of the people, by the people, for the people, shall not perish from the earth.

ABRAHAM LINCOLN, in his Gettysburg Address (November 1863)

Speaking the truth in love,
we are to grow up in every way
into him who is the head, into Christ,

from whom the whole body, joined and knit together
by every joint with which it is supplied,
when each part is working properly,
makes bodily growth and upbuilds itself in love.

EPHESIANS 4:15–16

. . . with liberty and justice for all.
Pledge to the Flag

"We the People" still do not have complete control over our nation's institutions. COMMON CAUSE is a national citizen's movement working to make government on all levels more responsive to the people. It has more than 300,000 members active in every state. The members set the priorities in periodic referendums. COMMON CAUSE has worked on a variety of crucial issues: the protection of our environment, an end to U.S. military actions in Indochina, an end to discrimination based on race, sex, or ethnic background, freedom of information, the 18-year-old vote. But the issues that have become most distinctively "Common Cause issues" are those that determine whether politics and government will continue to be corrupted by money and secrecy, whether the political process will be responsive to the citizen-taxpayer, whether citizens can hold their government accountable. "COMMON CAUSE," writes *The*

Wall Street Journal, "has proved the skeptics and the cynics wrong. . . . It has demonstrated increasing clout on the toughest kind of reform issues . . . . COMMON CAUSE seems to offer a means to combat the 'sense of powerlessness' to influence government actions." For annual dues of $15 you will receive *Report from Washington* ten times a year and will be advised about crucial issues and how you can act on them. Their address is COMMON CAUSE, 2030 M Street, N.W., Washington, D.C. 20036.

THE NEW AMERICAN MOVEMENT (NAM) exists to help organize a movement for democratic socialism in the United States. Its aim is to establish working-class control of the enormous productive capacity of American industry, to create a society that will provide material comfort and security for all people, and in which the full and free development of every individual will be the basic goal. Such a society will strive for decentralization of decision making, an end to bureaucratic rule, and participation of all people in shaping their own lives and the direction of society. The organization believes that the elimination of sexist and racist institutions and the dismantling of American economic and social control abroad are central to the struggle. For more information and the address of the nearest local chapter, write THE NEW AMERICAN MOVEMENT, 2421 E. Franklin Avenue So., Minneapolis, Minnesota 55406.

A Public Citizen's Action Manual by Donald K. Ross with an introduction by Ralph Nader (New York: Grossman, 1973) provides information, ideas, models, and strategies for many of the problems or injustices that prevail throughout the country and that you can help prevent or diminish. Sections include: "How to Do a Bank Interest Survey," "How to Do a Toy Safety Survey," "How to Investigate Discrimination by Employment Agencies," "How to Discover Corporate Tax Dodges," "How to Improve Small Claims Courts," "How to Form a Citizen Action Group." The *Manual* is meant to generate a contagious enthusiasm for effective citizen involvement in community, state, and national problem solving.

6

*. . . in Order to form
a more perfect Union, . . .*

*Behold, how good and pleasant it is
when brothers dwell in unity!*

PSALM 133:1

We must love brotherly without dissimulation; we must love one another with a pure heart fervently; we must bear one another's burdens; we must not look only on our own things, but also on the things of our brethren.

> JOHN WINTHROP, first governor of Massachusetts Bay Colony, in a sermon aboard the *Arbella* (1630)

Let us then, fellow citizens, unite with one heart and one mind, let us restore to social intercourse that harmony and affection without which liberty and even life itself are but dreary things.

> THOMAS JEFFERSON, in his First Inaugural Address (March 1801)

*Now the company of those who believed
were of one heart and soul,
and no one said that any of the things
which he possessed was his own,
but they had everything in common.*

And with great power the apostles gave their testimony
to the resurrection of the Lord Jesus,
and great grace was upon them all.
There was not a needy person among them,
for as many as were possessors of land or houses sold them,
and brought the proceeds of what was sold
and laid it at the apostles' feet;
and distribution was made to each as any had need.

ACTS 4:32–35

The most common and durable source of faction has
been the various and unequal distribution of property.

JAMES MADISON, fourth president of the United
States, in *The Federalist*, no. 10 (1787)

Back in the '50's the gap between rich and poor seemed
to be narrowing, said speakers, and a series of hopeful
books hailed the supposed happy fact. Since then,
however, the marked disparity of income has not nar-
rowed but increased. Indeed, if the present boom slows
down, as widely expected, there may be rising unemployment, and a wider gap.

Let's take a statistic or two, offered by a team from
the Urban Institute and the Pennsylvania State
University—James D. Smith, Stephen D. Franklin
and Douglas A. Wion. They call the 4.4 percent of

property owners at the top of the population the "super-rich," and define them as those whose net worth is in excess of $60,000. Now most people living in detached homes on shady avenues in the suburbs don't think $60,000 makes them "super-rich" but that's just the point the speakers here made: there's a distorted notion of American income. The vocabulary doesn't fit the facts.

These 4.4 percent in 1969 held an estimated 35.6 percent of the nation's personally owned wealth. They owned 27 percent of all real estate, 40 percent of all noncorporate business assets, 60 percent of all personally held corporate stock and 77 percent of the state and local bonds (the lovely ones that are federally tax-exempt.) The top one-tenth of 1 percent of the adult population owned 62.8 percent of these tax-exempt bonds, the authors estimate, with a total of $8,981,600,000 of tax-exempt interest.

> *The Christian Science Monitor* (September 28, 1973)

Without judging anyone,
it has become clear to us
that the present economic order
does not care for its people.
In fact,
profit and people frequently are contradictory.

Profit over people is an idol . . . .
Great fortunes were built
on the exploitation of Appalachian workers
and Appalachian resources,
yet the land was left without revenues
to care for its social needs, like
—education
—welfare
—old age
—and illness.
Some may say,
"That's economics,"
but we say
that economics is made by people.
Its principles don't fall down from the sky
and remain for all eternity.
Those who claim
they are prisoners of the laws of economics,
only testify
that they are prisoners of the idol.
The same thing which is so obvious in Appalachia
goes on outside the mountains.
Plain people work hard all their life,
and their parents worked hard before them,
yet they can't make ends meet.
—Food is too expensive.
—Taxes are too high for most.
—(Too low for the rich).

—Sickness puts people into debt.
—College is out of reach for their children.
—Paychecks keep shrinking.
And it's worse still for those who can't work,
especially the elderly.
Meanwhile
corporate profits
for the giant conglomerates,
who control our energy resources,
keep on skyrocketing.

>   *This Land Is Home to Me,* A Pastoral Letter on
>   Powerlessness in Appalachia by the Catholic
>   Bishops of the Region (Lent 1975)

. . . in Order to form a more perfect Union . . .

Then the Lord said to Cain,
"Where is Abel your brother?"
He said, "I do not know; am I my brother's keeper?"
And the Lord said, "What have you done?
The voice of your brother's blood
is crying to me from the ground."

>   **GENESIS 4:9–10**

I have a dream that one day men will rise up and come
to see that they are made to live together as brothers. I

still have a dream this morning that one day every Negro in this country, every colored person in the world, will be judged on the basis of the content of his character rather than the color of his skin, and every man will respect the dignity and worth of human personality. I still have a dream today that one day the idle industries of Appalachia will be revitalized, and the empty stomachs of Mississippi will be filled, and brotherhood will be more than a few words at the end of a prayer, but rather the first order of business on every legislative agenda.

> MARTIN LUTHER KING, JR., in *The Trumpet of Conscience* (1967), p. 77

God grant that not only the love of liberty but a thorough knowledge of the rights of man may pervade all the nations of the earth, so that a philosopher may set his foot anywhere on its surface and say: "This is my country."

> BENJAMIN FRANKLIN, statesman, author, scientist, in a letter to David Hartley (December 1789)

I am ready to say to every human being "thou art my brother" and to offer him the hand of concord and amity.

> THOMAS JEFFERSON, in a letter to Brazer (1819)

Speaking the truth in love,
we are to grow up in every way
into him who is the head,
into Christ,
from whom the whole body,
joined and knit together
by every joint with which it is supplied,
when each part is working properly,
makes bodily growth and upbuilds itself in love.

EPHESIANS 4:15–16

When indeed shall we learn that we are all related one to the other, that we are all members of one body? Until the spirit of love for our fellowmen, regardless of race, color or creed, shall fill the world, making real in our lives and our deeds the actuality of human brotherhood—until the great mass of the people shall be filled with the sense of responsibility for each other's welfare, social justice can never be attained.

HELEN KELLER, in "To the Strikers at Little Falls, New York" (November 1912)

Nationalism is an infantile disease. It is the measles of mankind.

ALBERT EINSTEIN, in a statement to G.S. Viereck (1921)

Now it is possible for patriotism to fall from its high estate. Instead of calling men to wider horizons, it can keep them within narrow ones. Once the issue was patriotism versus a small parochialism; now the question may become patriotism versus a large care for humanity. Once patriotism was the great enemy of provincialism; now it can be made to mean provincialism and to sanctify the narrow mind . . . .

Two generations ago one of our great statesmen, Charles Sumner, said, "Not that I love country less, but Humanity more, do I now and here plead the cause of a higher and truer patriotism. I cannot forget that we are men by a more sacred bond than we are citizens —that we are children of a common Father more than we are Americans." Shall not each one of us here pray for his own country, as I pray earnestly for mine, that that spirit may come into the ascendency? Christianity essentially involves it.

> HARRY EMERSON FOSDICK, clergyman, orator, in an address to League of Nations delegates (September 1925)

. . . in Order to form a more perfect Union . . .

If peace is to come, nation-worship must be supplanted by the loyalty implicit in the declaration, "God so loved the world . . . " The individual is normally a patriot. We love the soil of our native land and the heritage that has shaped our days. Grateful for home and heritage we are now called to a higher patriotism. Once women and men were forced to organize as tribes for self-protection, then tribes as city-states and city-states as nation-states. Today we are called to look beyond the limited and competing boundaries of nation-states to the larger and more inclusive community of humanity.

> *The Bishops' Call for Peace and the Self-Development of Peoples*, adopted by the General Conference of the United Methodist Church, Atlanta, Georgia (April 1972)

"Am I my brother's keeper?"

GENESIS 4:9

During the reckless economic expansion of the last 300 years, the maritime peoples of Western Europe spread first their trade and then their investment all round the world, taking over all the temperate land, opening up colonial mines and plantations and weaving a web of commerce that made the cocoa farmer in Ashanti dependent upon the purchase of chocolate milk shakes in New York, and the Arab bedouin on the fortunes of

Mr. Henry Ford. This tight mesh of economic interdependence has survived the ending of political colonial control. The two-thirds of humanity in ex-colonial lands still depend very heavily on the third who are already developed, and meanwhile, new forms of international activity are appearing—for instance, the international corporations which manufacture the equivalent of a quarter of America's gross national product outside the United States and whose aim, stated or covert, is to produce goods where labour costs are lowest and hold profits where taxation is least, thus producing an "optimum" economic mix that may bear little or no relation to the social needs of local communities.

There is, therefore, an economic "continuum" at the planetary level in which the nations have to work to resolve traditional issues like distribution, social justice or inflation, and confront such new issues as the risk that technological breakdown may follow or pollution and the exhaustion of resources. In other words, urgent economic problems require solutions which can only be achieved at a planetary level. But the means of solving them are still in the hands of national governments. We live physically and socially in a postnational order. But we still worship "the idols of the tribe."

> BARBARA WARD, in *A New Creation?: Reflections on the Environmental Issue* (1973), pp. 24–25

Think of our world as it looks from the rocket that is heading toward Mars. It is like a child's globe, hanging in space, the continents stuck to its side like colored maps. We are all fellow passengers on a dot of earth.

> LYNDON B. JOHNSON, thirty-sixth president of the United States, in his Inaugural Address (January 1965)

Is our spacecraft really hurtling toward massive human disaster: cataclysmic human upheaval and the reduction of this beautiful globe to a burned-out cinder? One can be optimistic, I believe, only if this generation—the young particularly—can shuck off the madness of the nightmare that man for centuries, and increasingly of late, has been living. A new vision is needed if man is to create on earth the beauty that this planet manifests from afar. The vision must be one of social justice, of the interdependence of all mankind. Unless the equality, the oneness, and the common dignity of mankind pervade the vision, the only future of this planet is violence and destruction on an ever increasing scale—a crescendo of inhumanity that can only result in total destruction. As a young man in the Peace Corps in Malawi, Africa, put it, "While our leaders have their power battles and ego trips, countless millions of unknowns are in need of a bit more food, a year or two more of education, another pot or pan, a sensible way of controlling family size, a book or a bicycle. These people aren't asking for much; they would only like to be a bit more free to be a bit more human."

I believe that none but the young—and the young in heart—can dream this vision or pursue this ideal, for it means leaving behind the conventional wisdom that pervades the aging bones of the Western world.

THEODORE M. HESBURGH, in *The Humane Imperative* (1974), p. 103

It is a fact that, as yet, no Western developed nation has made any real sacrifices in shouldering aid obligations to underdeveloped countries. Neither have they been prepared, on the whole, to abstain from even minor trading advantages that can be shown not to be of real long-term interest to a developed country. The trend has not gone in the direction of greater willingness to come to the assistance of the underdeveloped countries.

GUNNAR MYRDAL, in *The Challenge of World Poverty* (1970), p. 313

The tension between national self-interest and the global human community tears the fabric of the brotherhood of man and produces the intolerable dichotomy of rich and poor nations. People suffer. As the major economic power in the world, America is prone to define its national interests in terms of protecting its economic position.

> CARROLL T. DOZIER, Catholic Bishop of Memphis, in his pastoral letter "Justice: God's Vision, Man's Discipleship" (December 1972)

. . . in Order to form a more perfect Union . . .

Beloved, I am writing you no new commandment,
but an old commandment
which you had from the beginning;
the old commandment is the word which you have heard.
Yet I am writing you a new commandment,
which is true in him and in you,
because the darkness is passing away
and the true light is already shining.
He who says he is in the light and hates his brother
is in the darkness still.
He who loves his brother abides in the light,
and in it there is no cause for stumbling.
But he who hates his brother
is in the darkness and walks in the darkness,
and does not know where he is going,
because the darkness has blinded his eyes.

JOHN 2:7–11

America! America! God shed His grace on thee,
And crown thy good with brotherhood,
From sea to shining sea!

> *America, the Beautiful* by Katherine Lee Bates
> (1895)

> **. . . with liberty and justice for all.**
> *Pledge to the Flag*

To be truly "a more perfect Union," the U.S. must eliminate the deep divisions existing in our country today. It is only by struggling against these injustices that we can move toward genuine unity. One group trying to overcome such injustice and division is the UNITED FARM WORKERS OF AMERICA.

America's 2.6 million farm workers are the lowest paid income group in the country. Many of them are migrants. They follow the crops from the Mexican border to the State of Washington, from Texas to Michigan, from Florida to New England; or they travel widely within one state. They are of all colors. They are poor.

A consumer boycott of non-UFWA grapes and lettuce is the only means this small union has to compel the growers to recognize their workers' right to have secret ballot elections to determine which union—if any —they want to represent them.

The future of the farm workers will be decided in local food stores or supermarkets. And the decision is yours to make.

1. Do not buy or eat California grapes or iceberg (head) lettuce until the growers recognize their workers' right to choose by secret ballot which union representation they want.

2. Raise the issue of the boycott at supermarkets, restaurants and wherever else grapes or lettuce are served or sold.

3. Help your local boycott committee or organize one of your own.

4. Arrange for talks on farm worker conditions to your organizations, churches, schools, home meetings.

5. Support legislation that affords farm workers the protections that other workers have.

6. Read articles about farm workers in newspapers, magazines and books.

7. Write letters to the editor in support of farm workers' rights.

8. For further ways to become involved contact: UNITED FARM WORKERS OF AMERICA, P.O. Box 62, Keene, California 93531; or the National Farm Worker Ministry, 1411 W. Olympic Blvd., Los Angeles, California 90015.

> (Adapted from the *News Notes* of The Christophers, 12 E. 48th Street, New York, New York 10017)

7

. . . establish Justice,
insure domestic Tranquillity, . . .

The Preamble of our Constitution does not speak merely of justice or merely of order; it embraces both. Two of the six purposes set forth in the Preamble are to "establish justice" and to "insure domestic tranquility."

> *To Establish Justice, To Insure Domestic Tranquility*,
> Final Report of the National Commission on the
> Causes and Prevention of Violence (December
> 1969), p. xxii

Justice will dwell in the wilderness,
and righteousness abide in the fruitful field.
And the effect of righteousness will be peace
and the result of righteousness, quietness and trust for ever.
My people will abide in a peaceful habitation,
in secure dwellings, and in quiet resting places.

> ISAIAH 32:16–18

Every person within this jurisdiction, whether inhabitant or foreigner, shall enjoy the same justice and law that is general for the plantation, which we constitute and execute one toward another without partiality or delay.

> *Massachusetts Body of Liberties* (1641), no. 2

. . . establish Justice . . .

Justice is justly represented Blind, because she sees no Difference in the Parties concerned.

She has but one Scale and Weight, for Rich and Poor, Great and Small.

Her Sentence is not guided by the Person, but the Cause . . . .

Impartiality is the Life of Justice, as that is of Government.

> WILLIAM PENN, in his *Some Fruits of Solitude* (1693), nos. 407–09, 411

You are now the guardians of your own liberties. We may justly address you, as the *decemviri* did the Romans, and say: "Nothing that we propose can pass into a law without your consent. Be yourselves, O Americans, the authors of those laws on which your happiness depends."

> SAMUEL ADAMS, propagandist, political figure, revolutionary leader, in a speech before the Continental Congress (August 1776)

It is to be regretted that the rich and powerful too often bend the acts of government to their selfish purposes. Distinctions in society will always exist under every just government. Equality of talents, of education, or of wealth can not be produced by human institutions. In the full enjoyment of the gifts of Heaven and the fruits of superior industry, economy, and virtue, every man is equally entitled to protection by law; but when the laws undertake to add to these natural and just advantages artificial distinctions, to grant titles, gratuities, and exclusive privileges, to make the rich richer and the potent more powerful, the humble members of society—the farmers, mechanics, and laborers—who have neither the time nor the means of securing like favors to themselves, have a right to complain of the injustice of their Government.

ANDREW JACKSON, seventh president of the United States, in his veto of the Bank Renewal Bill (July 1832)

Rigid and expeditious justice is the first safeguard of freedom, the basis of all ordered liberty, the vital force of progress. It must not come to be in our Republic that it can be defeated by the indifference of the citizen, by exploitation of the delays and entanglements of the law, or by combinations of criminals. Justice must not fail because the agencies of enforcement are either delinquent or inefficiently organized. To consider these evils, to find their remedy, is the most sore necessity of our times.

HERBERT HOOVER, thirty-first president of the United States, in his Inaugural Address (March 1929)

And the word of the Lord came to Zechariah, saying,
"Thus says the Lord of hosts, Render true judgements,
show kindness and mercy each to his brother,
do not oppress the widow, the fatherless,
the sojourner, or the poor."

ZECHARIAH 7:8–10

In 1970, the nineteen largest oil companies paid only 8.7 percent federal income tax on combined net incomes of almost $9 billion. A taxpayer with income of $10,000 paid 21% in taxes. In 1971, five large corporations—Continental Oil, McDonnell Douglas, Gulf and Western, Alcoa and the Signal Companies—paid no income tax at all on combined incomes of $380 million [Tax Reform Research Group, "People and Taxes," vol. 1, issue 9 (Washington, D.C.)].

The result of such tax inequities is to place the burden on workers and low income taxpayers. Economists at the Brookings Institute in Washington, D.C., have estimated that taxes could be cut by 43% across the board if such loopholes were closed. But until then the taxpayer must continue to pay the cost of corporate profit-making and expansion.

> *Corporate Action Guide*, published by the Corporate Action Project, Washington, D.C. (1974), p. 15

A new official report by the Internal Revenue Service discloses that many wealthy people still manage to pay little or no federal income tax . . . .

402 Americans with incomes of $100,000 or more in 1972 escaped federal taxes entirely—and four of them made than a million dollars.

U.S. News & World Report (June 3, 1974), p. 49

. . . establish Justice . . .

The Third World is all around us, even right here in "the good ole U.S. of A.," as Archie Bunker might say. West Virginia is a classic case—a domestic variety of a Third World country, with many of the symptoms that plague so-called poor countries of the world, like Bolivia, Ecuador and Indonesia.

The "Report of the President's Appalachia Regional Commission" puts the West Virginia scene in terms that are interchangeable with those describing much of the Third World. The report noted that where an area "depends primarily on the extraction of natural resources for its income and employment"—as is the case in West Virginia, Bolivia, Zambia, Namibia, etc.—"it is extremely important that a high proportion of wealth created by extraction be reinvested locally in other activities."

The fact is, "Much of the wealth produced by coal

and timber," as the Commission noted, "was seldom seen locally. It went downstream with the great hardwood logs; it rode out on the rails with the coal cars; it was mailed between distant cities as royalty checks from non-resident operators to holding companies who had bought rights to the land for fifty cents or a dollar an acre." . . .

West Virginia upsets conventional ideas about geography. Although a state—the 35th to join the Union —it is more correct to say it is an occupied colony, owned virtually lock, stock, and barrel by non-residents. Some of the world's major corporations, with incomes exceeding those of dozens of nations, own significant holdings in West Virginia. Although its people are poor—West Virginia ranks 44th in per capita income in the nation—until recently, it was the nation's major source of hardwood lumber and is still the chief supplier of bituminous coal.

To gain a perspective of the plight of West Virginia, it is helpful to visit a region 400 miles northwest of the State—the near-northside of Chicago. This section is a "suburb" of West Virginia, or more properly, a kind of resettlement camp for economic refugees from Appalachia. Here, in a squalor only a developed nation can produce, are hordes of marginal persons, ill-fed, inhumanly housed, illiterate and deprived of political power as well as of the means of acquiring responsibility and moral dignity.

If that kind of life represents to these Chicago-West

Virginians an escape from the oppressive conditions back home, then the situation in West Virginia must surely be abominable.

Although the unemployment gap between Appalachia and the rest of the nation is steadily closing, the grim fact is that West Virginia is exporting its unemployment. Deprived of any hope for a meaningful future, more that 700,000 West Virginians left the State in the last 20 years.

Like their propertyless brothers and sisters in Asia, Africa and Latin America, they flee from impoverished rural regions and dehumanizing mechanization and swarm into the barrios and ghettoes.

If the adjacent states had had passport restrictions and visa requirements inhibiting this mass migration, it is conceivable that war would have broken out in the Appalachian Mountains and the Ohio River Valley.

What adds irony to the tragedy of this American colony—West Virginia—is the motto emblazoned on the state's seal: "Montani Semper Liberi," i.e., "Mountaineers are always freemen."

> "The West Virginia Model," in *Justice in the World: A Primer for Teachers*, U.S. Catholic Conference, Division for Justice and Peace

Ironically, cane-worker poverty persists in a day when the sugar industry itself seems sweeter than ever. Because of a world-wide scarcity of sugar and increasing demand, American consumers are paying $2.17 for a five-pound bag of sugar, nearly three times the price of a year ago and the highest level in history. As a result, growers are expected to harvest a record profit. Despite Hurricane Carmen, which flattened 20% of the Louisiana crop last month, the state's cane this year is expected to bring a gross price of $383.6 million, or 149% more than last year's crop.

In the past, little of the industry profits, however, have filtered down to the workers. Witness the shoddy condition of the plantation housing, known as "quarters," in which most workers live. While Louisiana growers lately have spent considerable sums to improve the quarters—the number with indoor toilets, for example, has risen to 83% from 18% five years ago—deplorable housing still abounds in the state's 17-parish sugar belt.

The Adams family, for example, lives in a weathered, four-room shack about a half-mile from the plantation owner's spacious brick home, which is set in a grove of massive, ancient live-oak trees gracefully draped with Spanish moss.

The Wall Street Journal (October 17, 1974)

**. . . establish Justice,
insure domestic Tranquillity . . .**

Seek good, and not evil,
that you may live;
and so the Lord, the God of hosts,
will be with you, as you have said.
Hate evil, and love good,
and establish justice in the gate.

AMOS 5:14–15

I still have a dream today that one day justice will roll down like water, and righteousness like a mighty stream. I still have a dream today that in all of our state houses and city halls men will be elected to go there who will do justly and love mercy and walk humbly with their God.

MARTIN LUTHER KING, JR., in *The Trumpet of Conscience* (1967), p. 77

Our society has commissioned its police to patrol the streets, prevent crime, and arrest suspected criminals. It has established courts to conduct trials of accused offenders and sentence those who are found guilty. It has created a correctional process consisting of prisons to punish convicted persons and programs to rehabilitate and supervise them so that they can become useful citizens. It is commonly assumed that these three components—law enforcement (police, sheriffs, marshals), the judicial process (judges, prosecutors, defense lawyers) and corrections (prison officials, probation and parole officers)—add up to a "system" of criminal justice.

A system implies some unity of purpose and organized interrelationship among component parts. In the typical American city and state, and under federal jurisdiction as well, no such relationship exists. There is, instead, a reasonably well-defined criminal *process*, a continuum through which each accused offender may pass: from the hands of the police, to the jurisdiction of the courts, behind the walls of a prison, then back onto the street. The inefficiency, fall-out and failure of purpose during this process is notorious.

> *To Establish Justice, To Insure Domestic Tranquility*, Final Report of the National Commission on the Causes and Prevention of Violence (December 1969), p. 149

Remember those who are in prison,
as though in prison with them.

HEBREWS 13:3

Our Law says well, to delay Justice is Injustice.

> WILLIAM PENN, in his *Some Fruits of Solitude* (1693), no. 393

In regard to our penitentiaries, I have urged that discipline ought to be tempered with kindness, and that moral influences should be employed to secure the submission and promote the reformation of convicts. Although some improvement has been made in this respect, more can yet be accomplished. It is too often forgotten, that the object chiefly contemplated in the adoption of our penitentiary system, was the reformation of offenders. This object derives its importance from considerations of prudence, as well as of philanthropy. The unreformed convict, after being released, spends a brief period in committing depredations upon society, and in corrupting youth, and then returns to the prison to exercise a vicious influence upon his fellow-prisoners there. Reformation can seldom be expected, without addressing the mind. I would have the school-room in the prison fitted as carefully as the solitary cell and workshop; and although attendance there can not be so frequent, I would have it quite as regular.

> WILLIAM H. SEWARD, Governor of New York,
> in his Annual Message to the New York State
> Legislature (January 1841)

Criminal courts themselves are often poorly managed and severely criticized. They are seriously backlogged; in many of our major cities the average delay between arrest and trial is close to a year. All too many judges are perceived as being inconsiderate of waiting parties, police officers and citizen witnesses. Too often lower criminal courts tend to be operated more like turnstiles than tribunals. In some jurisdictions, many able jurists complain that some of their most senior colleagues refuse to consider or adopt new administrative and managerial systems which could improve significantly the quality of justice and the efficiency of the court and which would also shorten the time from arrest to trial.

> *To Establish Justice, To Insure Domestic Tranquility*,
> Final Report of the National Commission on the
> Causes and Prevention of Violence (December
> 1969), p. 151

We spend ninety-five cents of every dollar for prisons on pure custody; iron bars and stone walls; and they dehumanize. We spend five cents on hope—health, mental health and physical health, education, vocational training, employment services, family guidance, community services. Most of those inmates have never been to a dentist. Psychoses and neuroses among those people—a major cause of crime—are immense.

> RAMSEY CLARK, Attorney General of the United
> States, in a speech at Atlantic City (1970)

I was ill and you comforted me, in prison and you came to visit me. Then the just will ask him: "Lord

. . . when did we visit you when you were ill or
in prison?" The King will answer them: "I assure you,
as often as you did it for one of my least brothers, you
did it for me." (Matt. 25:36ff) . . .

In recent years Americans have experienced deepen-
ing concern over the presence and nature of crime in
our nation. We share this concern. Fully adequate law
enforcement and protection of law-abiding citizens are
clear but unmet needs. We oppose violence, whether in
defiance of law and order or under the cover of preserving law and order. We oppose both "crime in the
streets" and "white collar crime." Dedicated people
throughout the country are earnestly striving to iden-
tify and deal with the roots of crime. Some, very
properly, are questioning society's reaction to victim-
less crimes. Others are addressing themselves to the
issues of law enforcement and the procedures of our
criminal courts. Still others are concentrating their
attention upon the manner in which suspects and convicted criminals are dealt with and provided for while
incarcerated . . . .

It behooves us to be aware that, despite well-
publicized exceptions, prisons are largely filled with
the poor, the disadvantaged minorities, and the "los-
ers" of our society. We need to examine whether we
may not have a "poor man's " system of criminal justice. Often the petty thief—the shoplifter or the
pickpocket—goes to jail while the clever embezzler, the

glib swindler, the powerful racketeer, the polished profiteer may only undergo the litigation of the civil courts. In the case of the open "vices" prohibited by law, the "town drunk" is sentenced by a judge while the "country club alcoholic" is treated by a physician. We insist that punishment, in order to fulfill its proper purpose, must fit the nature of the crime; it must be considerate of the offender's human dignity; and it must be tempered by mercy and constantly aimed at reconciliation.

The Reform of Correctional Institutions in the 1970s, A Formal Statement of the United States Catholic Conference (November 1973), pp. 3–5

We easily recognize and abhor direct, "hot" violence, such as terrorist attacks, bombings of buildings, murders and rapes. It is harder for most of us to get upset about indirect or "cold" violence, which does not seem as spine-chilling, but is so real that from day to day it chips away at our rights. Conscious decisions perpetuating inferior education in poverty areas are cold violence; landlords who, while collecting rents, do nothing about the filth and rot in their slum holdings, commit cold violence; discrimination against women, and abandoning the elderly are forms of cold violence. Violence is done in the manipulation of minds, in wasteful misuse of the world's goods, in inadequate wages, in placing private interests over the common good.

> CARROLL T. DOZIER, Catholic Bishop of Memphis, in his pastoral letter "Justice: God's Vision, Man's Discipleship" (December 1972)

. . . establish Justice, insure domestic Tranquillity . . .

If welfare assistance is arbitrarily cut off, if a landlord flagrantly ignores housing codes, if a merchant demands payment under an unfair contract, the poor —like the rich—can go to court. Whether they find satisfaction there is another matter. The dockets of many lower courts are overcrowded, and cases are handled in assembly-line fashion, often by inexperienced or incompetent personnel. Too frequently courts having jurisdiction over landlord-tenant and small claims disputes serve the poor less well than their creditors; they tend to enforce printed-form contracts, without careful examination of the equity of the contracts or the good faith of the landlords and merchants who prepare them.

> *To Establish Justice, To Insure Domestic Tranquility*, Final Report of the National Commission on the Causes and Prevention of Violence (December 1969), p. 143

Behold my servant, whom I uphold,
my chosen, in whom my soul delights;
I have put my Spirit upon him,
he will bring forth justice to the nations. . . .
He will faithfully bring forth justice.
He will not fail or be discouraged
till he has established justice in the earth;
and the coastlands wait for his law.

ISAIAH 42:1,3-4

The national government must in some form exercise supervision over corporations engaged in interstate business—and all large corporations are engaged in interstate business—whether by license or otherwise, so as to permit us to deal with the far-reaching evils of over-capitalization.

THEODORE ROOSEVELT, in a speech at Washington, D.C. (April 1906)

Antitrust and *monopoly:* the words typically project antique images on our memory screens—a combative Teddy Roosevelt, industrial tycoons, corporate empires, victimized farmers. The old robber barons are gone, replaced by Harvard Business School types with forgettable names. (Who today would have the public nerve or unwisdom to utter, as did J.P. Morgan, "I owe the public nothing"?) The old trusts and monopolies themselves have largely disappeared, with more subtle variations—oligopolies and conglomerates—arising instead. And monopoly costs usually go unperceived by victims due to their remote and technical nature.

—An international quinine cartel cornered the world market in the early 1960s, then raised the price of quinine from 37 cents an ounce to $2.13. The drug, taken mostly by the elderly to restore natural heart rhythm, became priced beyond many patients' means. "I cannot continue to pay these high prices," complained one older citizen, "yet my doctor tells me I cannot live without it . . . . "

—Due to a conspiracy among nearly all the country's manufacturers of plumbing fixtures, homeowners and apartment dwellers overpaid for the sinks and toilets in the early Sixties. The firms had met secretly and decided to produce only the most expensive fixture models and charge a uniformly high price.

—In 1964 all Americans paid about 20 cents for a loaf of bread. But in Seattle they paid 24 cents, or 20% more, due to a local price-fixing conspiracy. After a Federal Trade Commission ruling ended the conspiracy, the Seattle price began to fall, reaching the national average by 1966. In its 10-year life, the conspiracy robbed consumers in the Seattle-Tacoma area of some $35 million . . . .

—Federal Trade Commission economists estimate that cold-cereal prices are inflated 15 to 20% because three giant firms (Kellogg, General Mills, and General

Foods) control 82% of the market and their high advertising expenditures (some 20% of sales) intimidate potential competitors.

> *The Closed Enterprise System*, Ralph Nader's
> Study Group Report on Antitrust Enforcement
> (1972), pp. 3–5

As through this world I've rambled,
I've seen lots of funny men.
Some rob you with a six-gun
and some with a fountain pen.

> WOODY GUTHRIE, composer and folk singer, in
> "Pretty Boy Floyd" (1958)

A merchant can hardly keep from wrongdoing,
and a tradesman will not be declared innocent of sin.
Many have committed sin for a trifle,
and whoever seeks to get rich will avert his eyes.
As a stake is driven firmly into a fissure between stones,
so sin is wedged in between selling and buying.

> SIRACH 26:29–27:2

When recognized for what it is, corporate crime is more
costly in both economic and social terms than street
crime. The street criminal dents our pocketbooks and
security. The business criminal, however, sabotages

our body politic, social ideals, and economic structure. For, unlike his street equivalent, he violates our trust and, consequently, inspires mistrust. If nothing else, the street robber usually robs from necessity and promises us nothing. The suite robber robs from want, after taking us into respectable confidence. "If the word 'subversive' refers to efforts to make fundamental changes in a social system," Edwin Sutherland once noted, "the business leaders are the most subversive influence in the United States."

> *The Closed Enterprise System*, Ralph Nader's Study Group Report on Antitrust Enforcement (1972), p. 147

. . . establish Justice, insure domestic Tranquillity . . .

The earth is the Lord's and the fulness thereof, the world and those who dwell therein.

PSALM 24:1

Aspen, Colorado

Still considered by some to be the single largest "constituency" in the nation, America's religious communities have again been challenged to take the leadership on an overriding moral issue. A decade ago, the issue was racial justice; this time it is *global* justice. Alarmed by the spreading famines in Africa and Asia, the disastrous consequences of the energy crisis and the spiraling world population, 125 religious leaders spent four tightly packed days here at the behest of the Overseas Development Council and the Aspen Institute for Humanistic Studies to be "conscienticized" about the potentially tragic future ahead for both the developing and developed worlds if countries such as the U.S. do not begin to alter their political and economic policies with a view toward long-range global justice.

Former Secretary of Defense Robert McNamara, presently head of the World Bank, voiced the hope of the sponsors when he told the gathering: "The church was guilty for a hundred years of failing to take the lead in securing justice for blacks. Must we wait another hundred years before the church makes the nation aware of the needs of the developing world?" McNamara, speaking as a Presbyterian elder, asked, "If the churches don't speak to these issues, who will?" Then McNamara, speaking as a statistical expert, reported that 800 million persons live on 30 cents a day or less, that 25 per cent of the developing world's children die before they are five years old and that life expectancy in those countries is at least 20 years shorter than in America. Developing countries, he said, will not achieve the modest established goal of a 6 per cent increase in Gross National Product, and will pay out as much in repayment of past loans as they will receive from new loans from the World Bank. Demonstrating that the United States has the capacity to increase its aid to developing countries without much sacrifice, McNamara observed that only 3 per cent of the expected U.S. growth in GNP through 1980 would be sufficient to enable the United States to come up at least to the U.N. established goal of .7 per cent of GNP in assistance funds. (Our nation now contributes only .125 per cent, earning for us 14th place among the 16 developed countries.) Quipped McNamara: "The poor will always be with us as long as we continue to act the way we have toward them." . . .

One day was spent in functional workshops organized around various strategies for getting the word out. The most significant document produced was a "Declaration of Conscience by Christians and Jews." Encompassing divergent views about political systems, the document nevertheless expressed the participants' unanimity on the basic issue:

> Our religious convictions compel us to take our stand on the side of the poor, the powerless and the oppressed. This is how we understand our obedience to God in this hour. This means, in effect, a commitment not merely to bring immediate relief to the suffering, but also to work toward the creation of global structures which will ensure basic dignity and humane existence for all people. This also means taking a stand against the present structures of society which prevent the kingdom of peace with justice from breaking in.

> *The Christian Century* (June 26, 1974)

Justice will dwell in the wilderness,
and righteousness abide in the fruitful field.
And the effect of righteousness will be peace
and the result of righteousness, quietness and trust for ever.
My people will abide in a peaceful habitation,
in secure dwellings, and in quiet resting places.

ISAIAH 32:16–18

. . . with liberty and justice for all.
Pledge to the Flag

One organization working to "establish justice" is the FRIENDS COMMITTEE ON NATIONAL LEGISLATION. FCNL is composed of Friends who feel a concern as Christians and as seekers after truth that the social, economic, and political aspects of life be conducted in love and justice. Governments, they believe, make decisions which result in war and peace, justice and injustice, and mankind's religious heritage and revelation should be brought to bear upon these decisions. The FCNL *Washington Newsletter* ($10 per year; $5 for those on limited income) carries legislative news of important issues that affect peace and justice. It also includes an analysis of the federal budget, the voting record of each member of Congress on key issues, and listings of major Committee and principal Subcommittee assignments. Write for their list of publications, including their How-To Series: "How to Write the Editor," "How to Work in Politics," "How to Visit Your Congressman," "How to Write Your Congressman and the President," "How to Work for the Congressional Candidate of Your Choice." FRIENDS COMMITTEE ON NATIONAL LEGISLATION is located at 245 Second Street, N.E., Washington, D.C. 20002.

THE LEAGUE OF WOMEN VOTERS is a nation-wide, grassroots organization which works toward a more just social order through legislative processes. On a local level, groups tackle such problems as housing, schools, environmental pollution. They lobby for programs they support and follow up to see to it that such programs are fairly and efficiently administered. State Leagues act to improve tax systems, to develop better elections laws and procedures, and to modernize state government. On the national level the League's voice is heard in Congress speaking for equality of opportunity in education, housing and employment; improved anti-pollution programs; building world cooperation through aid to developing nations and expanded trade. The members, in 1400 communities across the U.S., decide what issues they wish to study and take action on. And THE LEAGUE OF WOMEN VOTERS accepts male members. Write THE LEAGUE OF WOMEN VOTERS, 1730 M Street, N.W., Washington, D.C. 20036.

Corporate power can be subversive of our "domestic tranquillity" in ways much more damaging than street muggers. *The Corporate Examiner* is a publication which analyzes the most important information on corporate social responsibility culled from more than thirty business, financial, and trade journals and exclusive inside sources. It examines the actions and policies of major U.S. corporations in the areas of consumerism, environment, foreign investment, government, labor and minorities, military production, and corporate responsibility. It also carries news on institutional investor actions. It is available through the INTERFAITH CENTER ON CORPORATE RESPONSIBILITY, Rm. 566, 475 Riverside Drive, New York, New York 10027.

The *Corporate Action Guide*, a 105-page study guide on corporate power for concerned citizens, provides a key to understanding the many ways in which corporations wield tremendous power and influence over every aspect of our lives. A resource and organizing tool for concerted community action, it takes a close look at resources, alternatives, and people involved in action projects. The *Guide* is published by the CORPORATE ACTION PROJECT, an organization of people concerned about the impact of the corporate system on the distribution of wealth, resources, and power in the global community. Project members are committed to dialogue, education, action for change, and the creation of viable alternatives for a more just and human

society. For more information write CORPORATE ACTION
PROJECT, 1500 Farragut Street, N.W., Washington,
D.C. 20011.

Some of those who disturb our domestic tranquillity
we put in prison. The OFFENDER AID AND RESTORATION
(OAR) movement gives offenders a helping hand. OAR
volunteers go to school for three evenings of preparation. Then they go into the jail to enter the life of an
offender. You can help with money or with time. If
you cannot work in a jail, you can correspond with a
prisoner. If you give money, you enable OAR to recruit
and train more volunteers—and to provide more financial aid for the hosts of offenders who leave jail broke
and jobless. Write OFFENDER AID AND RESTORATION OF
U.S.A. (OAR-USA), 414 Fourth Street, N.E., Charlottes-
ville, Virginia 22901.

8

*. . . provide for
the common defence, . . .*

Blessed are the peacemakers,
for they shall be called sons of God.

MATTHEW 5:9

Were the money which it has cost to gain, at the close of a long war, a little town, or a little territory . . . , expended in improving what they already possess, in making roads, opening rivers, building ports, improving the arts, and finding employment for their idle poor, it would render them [the nations] much stronger, much wealthier and happier. This I hope will be our wisdom.

> THOMAS JEFFERSON, in his *Notes on Virginia*, Query 22 (1781)

I join with you most cordially in rejoicing at the return of peace. I hope it will be lasting, and that mankind will at length, as they call themselves reasonable creatures, have reason to settle their differences without cutting throats; for, in my opinion, there never was a good war or a bad peace.

> BENJAMIN FRANKLIN, statesman, author, scientist, in a letter to Josiah Quincy (1783)

Governments being in an uncivilized state and almost continually at war, they pervert the abundance which civilized life produces, to carry on the uncivilized part to a greater extent. By thus ingrafting the barbarism of government upon the internal civilization of a country, it draws from the latter, and more especially from the poor, a great portion of those earnings which should be applied to their own subsistence and comfort. Apart from all reflections of morality and philosophy, it is a melancholy fact that more than one fourth of the labor of mankind is annually consumed by this barbarous system.

THOMAS PAINE, in *The Rights of Man* (1791)

Hence, likewise, they [the parts of the Union] will avoid the necessity of those overgrown military establishments, which, under any form of government, are inauspicious to liberty, and which are to be regarded as particularly hostile to republican liberty.

GEORGE WASHINGTON, in his Farewell Address (September 1796)

The spirit of this country is totally adverse to a large military force.

THOMAS JEFFERSON, in a letter to Chandler Price (1807)

. . . provide for the common defence . . .

Adding up the months during which U.S. military forces were engaged in action—starting from the Revolutionary War and including wars against the Indians, punitive expeditions to Latin America and Asia, as well as major wars—we find that the United States was engaged in warlike activity during three-fourths of its history, in 1,782 of the last 2,340 months.

HARRY MAGDOFF, economist, in *American Economic Review* (May 1969), p. 237

You shall not kill.

EXODUS 20:13

There was about forty or forty-five people that we gathered in the center of the village . . . men, women, children . . . babies. And we all huddled them up . . . Lieutenant Calley . . . started shooting them. And he told me to start shooting. So I started shooting. I poured about four clips into the group. . . . I fired them on automatic . . . you just spray the area . . . so you can't know how many you killed. . . . I might have killed ten or fifteen of them . . . so we started to gather them up, more people, and we had seven or eight people. . . . We put them in the hootch, and we dropped a hand grenade in there with them. . . . They had about seventy or seventy-five people all gathered up. So we threw ours in with them and Lieutenant Calley . . . started pushing them off and shooting . . . off into the ravine. It was a ditch. And so we just pushed them off, and just started using automatics on them . . . men, women, children . . . and babies . . . . After I done it, I felt good, but later on that day it was gettin' to me. . . . It just seemed like it was the natural thing to do at the time.

> PAUL MEADLO, former private in the U.S. Army (Americal Division), in an interview on CBS-TV (November 24, 1969)

With the release last week of portions of the Pentagon report on the My Lai cover-up, Army Secretary Howard Callaway announced that "a dark chapter in the Army's history" had been concluded. There is little question that the whole episode, from the inception of the operation to the extremely belated release of the report, was an abysmal performance . . . . Secretary Callaway said, "It is an incident from which the Army has learned a great deal." Unfortunately, during the time of Watergate, the nation has also learned a great deal from My Lai and other current history. While the Army can change its training programs, Americans are left to wonder both about the integrity of their institutions and about a "system" in which so few are punished for such profoundly heinous and massively degrading crimes. It seems to us that such a chapter can never be concluded so long as conscience and memory remain.

> Editorial, *The New York Times* (November 22, 1974)

For the vineyard of the Lord of hosts is the house of Israel,
and the men of Judah are his pleasant planting;
and he looked for justice, but behold, bloodshed;
for righteousness, but behold, a cry!

ISAIAH 5:7

The Constitution of the United States, in the words of its preamble, was established, among other reasons, in order to "provide for the common defense, promote the general welfare, and secure the blessings of liberty." In the past generation the emphasis of our public policy has been heavily weighted on measures for the common defense to the considerable neglect of programs for promoting the liberty and welfare of our people . . . .

It may be that the people and their representatives are making a carefully reasoned sacrifice of welfare to security. It may be, but I doubt it. The sacrifice is

made so eagerly as to cause one to suspect that it is
fairly painless, that indeed the American people prefer
military rockets to public schools and flights to the
moon to urban renewal . . . .

> JOHN W. FULBRIGHT, U.S. Senator from
> Arkansas, in an address at the University of
> North Carolina (1964)

This year in our national budget the Congress has been
asked to approve the largest peacetime military budget
in our history. Over $90 billion dollars will be spent on
weapons of destruction and for the support of our
armies, including over half a million men stationed
permanently outside our borders. This total of military
expenditures amounts to 63 per cent of the funds Congress can actually control and is being asked to spend
this year.

By contrast, all the funds proposed in this year's
budget for the purpose of providing humanitarian and
economic assistance to other nations and to disadvantaged people comes to $1.9 billion. Much of this
money, in my opinion, is utilized more to gain political
influence than to relieve human suffering. This gives
us some idea of how we as a nation are exercising the
stewardship of our resources. It comes down to this:
For $1.00 that is spent in our nation's attempts to

alleviate suffering and enhance human life throughout the world, we spend $50.00 for the weapons and forces geared to the destruction of life.

MARK O. HATFIELD, U.S. Senator from Oregon, in *Worldview* (October 1974), p. 53

Following is a list of some civilian national needs not being met and their cost equivalents in military expenditures:

66 low-cost houses =
   $1 million = 1 Huey helicopter
Graduate fellowships funding cut, 1973 =
   $175 million = 1 nuclear aircraft carrier
National solid-waste-treatment program =
   $43.5 billion = B-1 bomber program
Child-nutrition programs funding cut =
   $69 million = 2 DE-1052 destroyer escorts
To eliminate hunger in America =
   $4-5 billion = C-5A aircraft program

The New York Times (December 4, 1974), adapted from *The Permanent War Economy* by SEYMOUR MELMAN, Professor of Industrial Engineering at Columbia University

Every gun that is made, every warship launched, every rocket fired signifies, in the final sense, a theft from those who hunger and are not fed, those who are cold and not clothed.

> DWIGHT D. EISENHOWER, in his "Cross of Iron" speech (April 1953)

Last night in a slum on the outskirts of La Paz, Bolivia, I saw a 25-year-old mother of two young children die in the arms of her husband because she did not have eight pesos (40 cents) to visit a doctor.

This morning, just as every other morning for the past year, 85 children met for classes in an empty lot because we do not yet have enough money available to build a school.

This afternoon, I saw a 47-year-old man cry because he could not afford to buy the food needed for his wife and five children.

Tonight I heard on the radio that the President of my country is asking Congress for some $85 billion for "defense spending." Before trying to sleep tonight, I have a very serious question to ask myself and the people of my country: Why?

> ROY BOURGEOIS, missionary, in *Maryknoll Magazine* (August 1974), p. 14

. . . **provide for the common defence** . . .

Have unity of spirit, sympathy,
love of the brethren,
a tender heart and a humble mind.
Do not return evil for evil
or reviling for reviling;
but on the contrary bless,
for to this you have been called,
that you may obtain a blessing. For
"He that would love life and see good days,
let him keep his tongue from evil
and his lips from speaking guile;
let him turn away from evil
and do right;
let him seek peace and pursue it."

I PETER 3:8–11

Religion, humanity, and policy all require the establishment of some peaceful means for the administration of international justice, and that they still further require the general disarming of the Christian nations, to the end that the enormous expenditures now lavished upon the War System may be applied to purposes of usefulness and beneficence, and that the business of the soldier may finally cease.

CHARLES SUMNER, U.S. Senator from Massachusetts, in an address to the American Peace Society (May 1849)

War should never be entered upon until every agency of peace has failed; peace is preferable to war in almost every contingency. Arbitration is the true method of settlement of international as well as local or individual differences.

> WILLIAM McKINLEY, twenty-fifth president of the United States, in his First Inaugural Address (March 1897)

I am anxious to bring home to you that the world is no longer country-size, no longer state-size, no longer nation-size. It is one world, as Willkie said. It is a world in which we must all get along. It will be just as easy for nations to get along in a republic of the world as it is for us to get along in the republic of the United States. Now, if Kansas and Colorado have a quarrel over a watershed they don't call out the National Guard of each State and go to war over it. They bring suit in the Supreme Court and abide by its decision. There isn't a reason in the world why we can't do that internationally.

> HARRY S. TRUMAN, in an address at the University of Kansas City (June 1945)

I know war as few other men now living know it, and nothing to me is more revolting. I have long advocated its complete abolition, as its very destructiveness on both friend and foe has rendered it useless as a means of settling international disputes.

> DOUGLAS MACARTHUR, General of the Army, in an address to a Joint Session of Congress (April 1951)

O Lord our Father, our young patriots, idols of our hearts, go forth to battle—be Thou near them! With them, in spirit, we also go forth from the sweet peace of our beloved firesides to smite the foe. O Lord our God, help us to tear their soldiers to bloody shreds with our shells; help us to cover their smiling fields with the pale forms of their patriot dead; help us to drown the thunder of the guns with the shrieks of their wounded, writhing in pain; help us to lay waste their humble homes with a hurricane of fire; help us to wring the hearts of their unoffending widows with unavailing grief; help us to turn them out roofless with their little children to wander unfriended the wastes of their desolated land in rags and hunger and thirst, sports of the sun flames of summer and the icy winds of winter, broken in spirit, worn with travail, imploring Thee for the refuge of the grave and denied it—for our sakes who adore Thee, Lord, blast their hopes, blight their lives, protract their bitter pilgrimage, make heavy their steps, water their way with their tears, stain the white snow with the blood of their wounded feet! We ask it, in the spirit of love, of Him Who is the Source of Love, and Who is the ever-faithful refuge and friend of all that are sore beset and seek His aid with humble and contrite hearts. Amen.

> MARK TWAIN, author and humorist, in "The War Prayer," first published posthumously in *Europe and Elsewhere* (1923)

In the councils of government, we must guard against the acquisition of unwarranted influence, whether sought or unsought, by the military-industrial complex. The potential for the disastrous rise of misplaced power exists and will persist.

> DWIGHT D. EISENHOWER, in his Farewell Address over radio and television (January 1961)

There is astonishingly little popular pressure for disarmament. The peace organizations are extremely weak everywhere and particularly so in the two countries which are running the armaments race. But there are everywhere strongly organized nationalist groups pleading against lowering the guard.

And the military-industrial complex represents a tremendously powerful combine of vested interests, resisting any serious move toward curbing the armaments race—particularly since it has now also involved many universities and actually become a military-industrial-academic complex. In some periods it almost seemed to have taken over the government in the United States.

GUNNAR MYRDAL, in *The Challenge of World Poverty* (1970), p. 314

Military expenditures for the world as a whole added up to an estimated total of $1,870 billion (at 1970 values) over the period 1961 to 1970 inclusive . . . . Military expenditures are in fact now running at two and a half times what all Governments are spending on health, one and a half times what they spend on education, and 30 times more than the total of all official economic aid granted by developed to developing countries. The economic scale of current world military expenditures can be realized even more dramatically when one remembers that they all but equal the combined GNP of the United Kingdom and Italy, or that of the developing countries of South Asia, the Far East and Africa together, with a total population of 1,300 million.

Economic and Social Consequences of the Arms Race and of Military Expenditures, Report of the Secretary-General, United Nations, New York (1972), p. 7

The United States sold some $8.5-billion in arms for the fiscal year that ended last month, almost double the arms sales for the previous fiscal year and almost $2-billion more than all the arms sold or given away by all nations in 1971, according to official Pentagon estimates . . . .

While the United States remains the world's leading arms supplier, other nations are also selling more . . . .

Arms control experts in the Government estimate that worldwide arms sales in the nineteen-seventies thus far have about equaled total arms sales for all of the sixties, even discounting for inflation.

The New York Times (July 10, 1974)

I look upon the whole world as my fatherland, and every war has to me a horror of a family feud. I look upon true patriotism as the brotherhood of man and the service of all to all. The only fighting that saves is the one that helps the world toward liberty, justice and an abundant life for all.

HELEN KELLER, in a speech at New York City (December 1915)

But the wisdom from above is first pure,
then peaceable, gentle, open to reason,
full of mercy and good fruits,

without uncertainty or insincerity.
And the harvest of righteousness is sown in peace
by those who make peace.
What causes wars,
and what causes fightings among you?
Is it not your passions that are at war in your members?
You desire and do not have; so you kill.
And you covet and cannot obtain,
so you fight and wage war.

JAMES 3:17–4:2

War is one of the constants of history, and has not diminished with civilization or democracy. In the last 3,421 years of recorded history only 268 have seen no war . . . .

The causes of war are the same as the causes of competition among individuals: acquisitiveness, pugnacity, and pride; the desire for food, land, materials, fuels, mastery. The state has our instincts without our restraints.

> WILL AND ARIEL DURANT, historians, in *The Lessons of History* (1968)

St. Paul knew enough about the forces of evil to know that they could be conquered only by greater *forces*, and so he set forth his famous method—"overcome evil with good." There is no other way to overcome it.

Something else, something better, must be put in its place . . . .

We shall not get very far with phrases like "passive resistance" or "non-resistance," or "the use of force is immoral." One can neither train a life nor build a world on those or any other slogans . . . . There would be little use having our Government and all the other governments of the world adopt abstract resolutions to the effect that military force shall be outlawed and shall never be resorted to again, if at the same time all the selfish and unjust methods of life and business and social relations were left to work just as they are now working. War is a fruit which grows and ripens like other fruit. No magic phrase, no written scrap of paper, will stop the ripening of it if the tree which bears it is planted and watered and kept in the sunshine and warm air. The axe must first be laid to the root of the tree.

RUFUS JONES, Quaker philosopher, in *The New Quest* (1928)

There are a thousand hacking at the branches of evil to one who is striking at the root.

HENRY DAVID THOREAU, in *Walden* (1854)

I still have a dream today that one day war will come to an end, that men will beat their swords into plowshares and their spears into pruning hooks, that nations will no longer rise up against nations, neither will they study war any more. I still have a dream today that one day the lamb and the lion will lie down together and every man will sit under his own vine and fig tree and none shall be afraid.

> MARTIN LUTHER KING, JR., in *The Trumpet of Conscience* (1967), p. 77

The land of the free, and the home of the brave.

> *The Star-Spangled Banner* by Francis Scott Key (1814)

. . . with liberty and justice for all.
Pledge to the Flag

Many U.S. citizens believe that our provision for the common defense has become inordinate. For example, SANE, A CITIZENS' ORGANIZATION FOR A SANE WORLD, promotes negotiated settlement of international disputes, major cuts in arms spending, transfer of resources to civilian programs, planning for the conversion of military bases and the arms industry, disarmament agreements, and strengthened international agencies. The organization distributes millions of

pieces of literature, publishes *Sane World,* and provides
educational materials and speakers. It mobilizes political effectiveness by maintaining contact with Congressional representatives and the Executive Department,
advising citizens on key issues through its Washington
office, and stimulating action in local communities. It
works closely with U.N. officials and U.N. delega-
tions. Local SANE groups conduct public meetings,
provide speakers, write letters, visit policy makers, and
support selected political candidates. Write SANE, 318
Massachusetts Ave., N.E., Washington, D.C. 20002.

The FELLOWSHIP OF RECONCILIATION invites you to
join them in FOR THE VICTIMS, a project of continuing
help to the victims of war extended via men and women
who share a commitment to nonviolence and reconciliation. How does the project work? Special collections.
Special worship services. Modification of normal worship services, "Meals of reconciliation"—gatherings for
prayer, readings and meditation centered around a
symbolic meal of tea and rice, signifying communion
with the victims of war in Asia. "Beg-ins"—collecting
contributions door-to-door or on street corners. Study
groups. A special FOR THE VICTIMS committee, a project
to encourage families and individuals in the churches
to sponsor particular orphans being helped by the
School of Youth for Social Service. Working for the
release of prisoners of conscience in Vietnam and other
countries—thus making direct connections between

the efforts to relieve suffering and efforts to get at the *causes* of suffering . . . . Two-thirds of the money collected in response to FOR THE VICTIMS will be shared with orphans, refugees and political prisoners in Vietnam; the balance will go into work for amnesty and the national and international peace efforts of the FELLOWSHIP OF RECONCILIATION. For more information write FELLOWSHIP OF RECONCILIATION, Box 271, Nyack, New York 10960.

THE UNITED STATES CATHOLIC CONFERENCE DIVISION OF JUSTICE AND PEACE has available a variety of peace education materials. Their publications list can be obtained by writing to 1312 Massachusetts Avenue, N.W., Washington, D.C. 20005.

9

*. . . promote
the general Welfare, . . .*

*Let each of you
look not only to his own interests,
but also to the interests of others.*

PHILIPPIANS 2:4

Salus populi suprema lex esto (Let the welfare of the people
be the supreme law).

State Motto of Missouri

Private property therefore is a creature of society and is
subject to the calls of that society whenever its necessities shall require it, even to its last farthing.

BENJAMIN FRANKLIN, in "On the Legislative
Branch" (1789)

There are in every country some magnificent charities
established by individuals. It is, however, but little
that any individual can do when the whole extent of the
misery to be relieved is considered. He may satisfy his
conscience, but not his heart. He may give all that he
has, and that all will relieve but little. It is only by
organizing civilization upon such principles as to act
like a system of pulleys, that the whole weight of
misery can be removed . . . .

It is the practice of what has unjustly obtained the

name of civilization (and the practice merits not to be called either charity or policy) to make some provisions for persons becoming poor and wretched only at the time they become so. Would it not, even as a matter of economy, be far better to devise means to prevent their becoming poor?

THOMAS PAINE, in *Agrarian Justice* (1797)

Why is it that willing hands are denied the prerogatives of labor, that the hand of man is against man? At the bidding of a single hand thousands rush to produce, or hang idle. Amazing that hands which produce nothing should be exalted and jeweled with authority! In yonder town the textile mills are idle, and the people want shoes. Fifty miles away, in another town, the shoe factories are silent, and the people want clothes. Between these two arrested forces of production is that record of profits and losses called *the market*. The buyers of clothes and shoes in the market are the workers themselves; but they cannot buy what their hands have made. Is it not unjust that the hands of the world are not subject to the will of the workers, but are driven by the blind force of necessity to obey the will of the few? And who are these few? They are themselves the slaves of the market and the victims of necessity.

HELEN KELLER, in *American Magazine* (December 1912)

I understand it to be the fundamental proposition of American liberty that we do not desire special privilege, because we know special privilege will never comprehend the general welfare . . . .

So what we have to discuss is, not wrongs which individuals intentionally do—I do not believe there are a great many of those—but the wrongs of a system. I want to record my protest against any discussion of this matter which would seem to indicate that there are bodies of our fellow-citizens who are trying to grind us down and do us injustice. There are some men of that sort. I don't know how they sleep o'nights, but there are men of that kind. Thank God, they are not numerous. The truth is, we are all caught in a great economic system which is heartless. The modern corporation is not engaged in business as an individual. When we deal with it, we deal with an impersonal element, an immaterial piece of society.

WOODROW WILSON, in *The New Freedom* (1913)

The property of the country belongs to the people of the country. Their title is absolute.

CALVIN COOLIDGE, thirtieth president of the United States, in his Inaugural Address (March 1925)

. . . promote the general Welfare . . .

The question is one of institutional structure, not individual morals. The political power of corporations does not depend upon bribes and illegal pressure tactics. It results from the use of legal tools only available to concentration of financial power. Corporate power in politics is the use of campaign contributions to elect pro-big business politicians, the use of advertising to sell political views rather than products, the use of tax deductible lobbying to make a case to Congress in ways beyond the reach of the average citizen, and the use of job opportunities to discourage tough regulation. All of these methods are legal but contrary to the public interest.

FRED R. HARRIS, U.S. Senator from Oklahoma,
in *Corporate Power in America* (1973), pp. 35–36

A number of years ago, scientists in one of the country's leading international companies happened upon a laboratory process for making a new type of fertilizer that held real promise for greatly expanding rice production. Successful development would clearly be enormously important for saving literally millions of lives throughout the underdeveloped world. When the company scientists reported the new discovery to corporate management and proposed to develop the fertilizer for this purpose, they were told to drop this approach. Instead, their scientific work was reorganized along the lines of developing the fertilizer for making greener lawn grass in the United States! The reason was that calculations showed the potential buying power of Americans desiring a more verdant lawn was far greater than that of impoverished peasants needing improved fertilizers. Thus, as soon as the data pointed out the correct direction for profit maximization, corporate management redirected the technostructure's work to meet that goal.

> MICHAEL TANZER, political economist, in *The Sick Society: An Economic Analysis* (1968), p.22

Soap and detergent firms spend some 20% of all sales revenues on ads, and drug houses spend *four times* more on advertising than on research. Once the product is made to seem sexier or faster or groovier, the seller can price it above the other brands, confident that consumers will continue to buy from him because a sense of "brand name" loyalty has been developed. "Competition" in gadgetry, trading stamps, style, and clever ads replaces price competition. Haven't we all pulled into an Esso station, bypassing something called Red Sky Gas, or bought Noxzema Shave Cream rather than the drab A&P brand? After all, Esso puts a "tiger in your tank" and Noxzema promises to "take it off, take it all off."

> *The Closed Enterprise System*, Ralph Nader's Study Group Report on Antitrust Enforcement (1972), p. 13

In a land of great wealth, families must not live in hopeless poverty. In a land rich in harvest, children just must not go hungry.

In a land of healing miracles, neighbors must not suffer and die unattended.

In a great land of learning and scholars, young people must be taught to read and write.

> LYNDON B. JOHNSON, in his Inaugural Address
> (January 1965)

I will rejoice in Jerusalem, and be glad in my people;
no more shall be heard in it the sound of weeping
and the cry of distress.
No more shall there be in it
an infant that lives but a few days,
or an old man who does not fill out his days,
for the child shall die a hundred years old.

> ISAIAH 65:19–20

Health is the first requisite after morality.

> THOMAS JEFFERSON, in a letter to Peter Carr
> (August 1787)

I am shocked to find that we in America have created a health care system that can be so callous to human suffering, so intent on high salaries and profits, and so unconcerned for the needs of our people. American families, regardless of income, are offered health care of uncertain quality, at inflated prices, and at a time and in a manner and a place more suited to the convenience and profit of the doctor and the hospital than to the needs of the patient. Our system especially victimizes Americans whose age, health, or low income leaves them less able to fight their way into the health care system. The health care industry seems by its nature to give most freedom and power to the providers of care—and very little to the people. It is an industry in which there is very little incentive to offer services responsive to the people's needs and demands. It is an industry which strongly protects the profit and rights of the provider, but only weakly protects the healing and the rights of the people . . . .

Every child who is retarded or whose arms or legs remain twisted because his parents could not get care, every family that faces financial disaster because of the cost of illness or is broken by unnecessary suffering or death, is kept from fulfilling the right to life, liberty, and the pursuit of happiness that we cherish in America.

EDWARD M. KENNEDY, U.S. Senator from Massachusetts, in *In Critical Condition: The Crisis in America's Health Care* (1972)

. . . promote the general Welfare . . .

The average income for the nation's 335,000 licensed doctors is $40,500 a year; only 1 per cent of Americans earn as much. But black babies in the slums still die of undiagnosed lead poisoning and sickle-cell anemia. And, while pharmaceutical corporations like Pfizer and Eli Lilly are making all-time record profits, lots of elderly citizens can't afford the inflated prices of prescription medicines.

There are publicized heart transplants and prestigious open heart surgery units in Houston's glittering medical complex. But Puerto Ricans still bleed to death in the dingy emergency waiting room of Lincoln Hospital in the South Bronx.

The United States is ahead of the rest of the world in medical technology and research. But America ranks fourteenth among industrial nations of the world in infant mortality rates, twelfth in maternal mortality, eighteenth in male life expectancy at birth, and eleventh for women.

In 1970, a nonpresidential year, the AMA contributed $700,000 to candidates opposed to national health insurance. But there are unhealthy children in Appalachia who haven't seen a doctor since they were born.

One simple syllogism seems to sum up health care in America. The poor get sick. The sick get poor. And the medical-industrial complex gets richer all the time.

> J. NEWFIELD AND J. GREENFIELD, in *A Populist Manifesto: The Making of a New Majority* (1972)

The recent discovery of fatal liver cancer among vinyl chloride workers has focused renewed attention of government, labor, industry and medicine on the thousands of known, suspected and as yet unsuspected health hazards that face 60 million working Americans . . . .

Historically, occupational health has been a low-priority item for both government and medicine.

Yet, each year one of every 10 workers suffers a job-related illness or injury. The Public Health Service estimates that prolonged on-the-job exposure to toxic chemicals, dusts, noise, heat, cold, radiation and other industrial conditions each year results in the death of at least 100,000 workers and the development of disabling occupational diseases in 390,000 more.

Researchers in occupational health believe that countless thousands of others succumb to insidious job related diseases not yet discovered by science.

The New York Times (March 4, 1974)

He coughed incessantly, and I shuddered each time I heard him. He doubled up, caught in an almost uncontrollable seizure. He growled and rumbled all the way down in his guts and brought up great gobs of mucus he spat directionlessly into the burnt-orange Florida earth. I could see the red flecks in the miniature puddles of dirt and excrement. Sometimes, self-consciously, he kicked dirt over the spit and covered it up. He didn't always think to do it; or he perhaps didn't give a damn.

That was Red. He had active, galloping tuberculosis and he had known it for a long time before I performed an on-the-spot lay diagnosis.

He had it; he knew it; and there was nothing he could do to get rid of it. That was the way of a seasonal, migratory farm laborer. Life—such as it was under the searing Florida sun—had to go on for Red, or the harvesters stooped over in the rows would go on without him, pushing and shoving their baskets before them as they struggled to scratch from the earth their meager existence.

> DALE WRIGHT, in *They Harvest Despair: The Migrant Farm Worker* (1965), pp. 6-7

The whole law is fulfilled in one word,
"You shall love your neighbor as yourself."
But if you bite and devour one another
take heed that you are not consumed by one another.

> GALATIANS 5:14–15

. . . promote the general Welfare . . .

Promote, then, as an object of primary importance institutions for the general diffusion of knowledge. In proportion as the structure of a government gives force to public opinion, it is essential that public opinion should be enlightened.

> GEORGE WASHINGTON, in his Farewell Address (September 1796)

The crippling of individuals I consider the worst evil of capitalism. Our whole educational system suffers from this evil. An exaggerated competitive attitude is inculcated into the student, who is trained to worship acquisitive success as a preparation for his future career.

> ALBERT EINSTEIN, theoretical physicist, in *Monthly Review* (May 1949)

Present-day education is still predicated on a number of myths: that the school or college is the exclusive place of education; that youth is the exclusive age of learning; that knowledge flows exclusively from the teacher; that education is properly measured by the accumulation of credits; that there is a rhythm or pattern of intellectual curiosity or social maturity common to all; that it is dangerous or counterproductive to mix young and old people in the same classrooms; that education must be experienced in unbroken sequences of 12 to 16 years; that prolonged adolescence is a good thing and that the more education one gets before working the better; that degrees and diplomas are the only indicators of talent and competence and the only instruments by which upward social and economic mobility may be acquired.

> EWALD B. NYQUIST, New York Commissioner of Education, in an address at Glens Falls, New York (October 1973)

. . . promote the general Welfare . . .

If your brother becomes poor,
and cannot maintain himself with you,
you shall maintain him.

> LEVITICUS 25:35

The welfare establishment and system in the United States is a monumental failure. It makes the taxpayer furious, it makes the welfare recipient bitter, and it inflicts the distillation of all this anger and bitterness on the children who will inherit this land. It is a disgrace to the American spirit.

> RICHARD M. NIXON, thirty-seventh president of the United States, in an address at Williamsburg, Virginia (April 1971)

The charge that costs of welfare programs for the poor are the reason for increasing tax burdens is greatly exaggerated. In fact, the United States as a whole now spends a lower percentage of its Gross National Product on welfare than it did in 1950.

By 1972, the percentage of the Gross National Product spent on all forms of public assistance (welfare to blind, aged, AFDC [Aid to Families with Dependent Children], etc.) equaled 2.3%.

For 1975, President Nixon requested more military expenditures than we've ever spent in history, *either in war* or *in peace*—about $11 billion more than last year. By 1980, the Pentagon plans to up this by 30% more!

The poor are victimized by a cultural value that considers military expenses of greater importance than greater social, economic, and political equality. Federal tax increases are much more related to military increases than to programs for the poor. As a society, *we are gradually spending less* of our wealth on government programs for the human development of the poor, not more as many people believe.

> *Poverty in American Democracy: A Study of Social Power*, United States Catholic Conference Campaign for Human Development (February 1975)

It would be interesting to compare welfare with other forms of American governmental subsidization as to cost and human justification. For openers, in nonwelfare costs, we subsidized others to the tune of $43-billion last year.

For example, we subsidize wealthy farmers; we subsidize railroads and airlines, and roads for those who have cars; we subsidize those looking for oil and gas, those investing in tax-free bonds, those sending heavy mail in huge quantities for commercial purposes; we subsidize military dictatorships, foreign investments, trips to the moon, travel by Congressmen and Government executives, everywhere for practically any purpose. We subsidize grain for the Russians and Chinese, even though it raises the cost of bread for our poor. We subsidize most poor countries while we gripe about a miserable subsidy to the poor of our own country, and cannot face the obvious solution: federalizing the program, providing work for those who can work and providing a minimal annual income for decent human living in America.

THEODORE M. HESBURGH, in *The New York Times Magazine* (October 29, 1972)

Bear one another's burdens,
and so fulfil the law of Christ.

GALATIANS 6:2

. . . with liberty and justice for all.
Pledge to the Flag

Volunteer groups provide numerous opportunities for those who want to become personally involved in "promoting the general welfare." THE COMMISSION ON VOLUNTARY SERVICE AND ACTION (CVSA) is a consultative council of more than one hundred and fifty private, North American organizations which sponsor and/or support voluntary service projects in all parts of the world. Their annual publication, *Invest Yourself*, provides the largest available listing of voluntary service projects and individual placement opportunities through North American organizations. It lists some 26,000 specific openings in several hundred projects. Write CVSA, Room 830, 475 Riverside Drive, New York, New York 10027.

THE HEALTH POLICY ADVISORY CENTER (HEALTH-PAC) is an independent research and education organization which provides data on patient's rights, health worker issues, community and worker struggles to change health institutions, the organization and financing of health care, Blue Cross, national health insurance proposals, and other health care topics. They also conduct workshops and supply technical assistance and speakers for community, worker, and student groups. Contact HEALTH-PAC, 17 Murray Street, New York, New York 10007.

NEW SCHOOLS EXCHANGE is a national clearinghouse for the exchange of ideas and information about alternatives in education. The group is in regular contact with persons and groups, community schools, free schools, innovative public schools, free universities, experimental colleges, learning exchanges, clearinghouses, networks. It publishes a monthly newsletter which contains articles and information about people/places/events/materials which are relevant to alternative education. It also publishes the only annual directory of alternative schools in the U.S. and Canada. Subscriptions to the newsletter (which includes the directory) are $10 a year for individuals, $12 for institutions and can be obtained from NEW SCHOOLS EXCHANGE, Pettigrew, Arkansas 72752.

Liberty and Justice for All: A Discussion Guide, a document designed particularly for parish group participation in the Bicentennial discussion, has been prepared by the National Conference of Catholic Bishops. The objective of the discussion guide is to introduce the Bicentennial program themes and topics to the Catholic community and to generate recommendations for the Church-sponsored Bicentennial Conference that is scheduled for 1976. A series of over 150 discussion questions on eight bicentennial topics is presented, raising issues that range from the use of Church property to crime in the streets. A response sheet is included at the end of the sixty-page document to record recommendations resulting from parish discussions during 1975. These recommendations can be forwarded to the NCCB Bicentennial Committee to form the basis for the 1976 conference. The guide also contains thirteen resource papers. It is available from the Publications Office of the U.S. Catholic Conference, 1312 Massachusetts Avenue, N.W., Washington, D.C. 20005.

Education for Justice: A Resource Manual has been written for Christian educators on all levels who want to design and conduct educational programs with justice as their focus. It contains an introduction to the various approaches to education for justice; background readings to orient the educator; twenty-one field-tested educational exercises in complete, self-contained units, dealing with stereotypes, viewpoints, power, critical sense, and other justice-related themes; guidelines for formulating one's own course of studies; and an extensive, annotated listing of additional resources available. The *Manual* has been designed for use with a *Participant Workbook*. Both are available (*Manual*, $7.95; *Workbook*, $3.95) from Orbis Books, Maryknoll, New York 10545.

10

. . . and secure
the Blessings of Liberty
to ourselves
and our Posterity, ...

I call heaven and earth to witness against you this day,
that I have set before you life and death,
blessing and curse;
therefore choose life,
that you and your descendants may live,
loving the Lord your God,
obeying his voice, and cleaving to him.

DEUTERONOMY 30:19–20

Love for his posterity spurs him [man] to exertion for their support, stimulates him to virtue for their example, and fills him with the tenderest solicitude for their welfare. Man . . . was made for all future times by the impulse of affection for his progeny.

> JOHN QUINCY ADAMS, sixth president of the United States, in an address at Plymouth, Massachusetts (December 1802)

Choose life,
that you and your descendants may live.

DEUTERONOMY 30:19

If there is any period one would desire to be born in, is it not the age of Revolution; when the old and the new stand side by side and admit of being compared; when the energies of all men are searched by fear and by hope; when the historic glories of the old can be compensated by the rich possibilities of the new era? This time, like all times, is a very good one, if we but know what to do with it.

> RALPH WALDO EMERSON, essayist and poet, in an address at Harvard University (August 1837)

The dogmas of the quiet past are inadequate to the stormy present. The occasion is piled high with difficulty, and we must rise with the occasion. As our case is new, so we must think anew, and act anew. We must disenthrall ourselves, and then we shall save our country.

> ABRAHAM LINCOLN, in his Annual Message to Congress (December 1862)

. . . and our Posterity . . .

In all my reading I am conscious of a multitudinous discontent. Slowly man is waking up. The people—the great "common herd"—are finding out what is wrong with the social, political and economical structure of the system of which they are a part.

This is not a time of gentleness, of timid beginnings

that steal into life with soft apologies and dainty grace. It is a time for loud-voiced, open speech and fearless thinking; a time of striving and conscious manhood, a time of all that is robust and vehement and bold; a time radiant with new ideals, new hopes of true democracy.

I love it, for it thrills me and gives me a feeling that I shall face great and terrible things. I am a child of my generation, and I rejoice that I live in such a splendidly disturbing time.

HELEN KELLER, in *Justice* (October 1913)

I do not believe that the Great Society is the ordered, changeless, and sterile battalion of the ants.

It is the excitement of becoming—always becoming, trying, probing, falling, resting, and trying again—but always trying and always gaining.

In each generation—with toil and tears—we have had to earn our heritage again.

LYNDON B. JOHNSON, in his Inaugural Address (January 1965)

Choose life,
that you and your descendants may live.

DEUTERONOMY 30:19

. . . and our Posterity . . .

Because we now know that the resources of the earth
are finite and that the biosphere is not infinitely forgiv-
ing, each generation must act as trustee for the next, or
at some point there will certainly be no next generation. We are the first generation to have the awareness
that man has the power to end history, and the first that
has the destructive technology to end it ourselves.

> RICHARD BARNET AND RONALD MÜLLER, in
> "Global Reach," *The New Yorker* (December 9,
> 1974), pp. 156–57

If a man walk in the woods for love of them half of each
day, he is in danger of being regarded as a loafer; but if
he spends his whole day as a speculator, shearing off
those woods and making earth bald before her time, he
is esteemed an industrious and enterprising citizen.

> HENRY DAVID THOREAU, in "Life Without Prin-
> ciple," first published posthumously in the *At-
> lantic Monthly* (1863)

With riches has come inexcusable waste. We have
squandered a great part of what we might have used,
and have not stopped to conserve the exceeding bounty
of nature, without which our genius for enterprise
would have been worthless and impotent.

> WOODROW WILSON, in his First Inaugural Ad-
> dress (March 1913)

The over-all level of environmental quality in the United States has sagged slightly in the last year, the nation's largest conservation organization says.

The slow pace of air and water pollution abatement, depletion of resources, and "uglification" of cities were among adverse factors cited by the National Wildlife Federation in its annual assessment of the country's liveability.

The New York Times (February 26, 1974)

Is it not enough for you to feed on the good pasture,
that you must tread down with your feet
the rest of your pasture;
and to drink of clear water,
that you must foul the rest with your feet?
And must my sheep eat
what you have trodden with your feet,
and drink what you have fouled with your feet?
Therefore, thus says the Lord God to them:
Behold, I, I myself will judge
between the fat sheep and the lean sheep.
Because you push with side and shoulder,
and thrust at all the weak with your horns,
till you have scattered them abroad,
I will save my flock,
they shall no longer be a prey;
and I will judge between sheep and sheep.

EZEKIEL 34:18–22

The United States with 6 percent of the earth's people consumes 35 percent of its resources.

Even American food intake is high-energy consuming. A poor Asian eats about 400 pounds of grain a year and little else. An American eats more than a ton—150 pounds directly as bread, pastries, and breakfast cereals but the rest indirectly as meat, milk, and eggs.

The resources needed to feed an American—land, water, and fertilizer—are five times those needed for an average Indian or Nigerian. And an American's overall energy consumption is 60 times greater.

Specific comparisons can turn up far greater extremes.

A poor Javanese eats rice, lights his house with coconut oil from a nearby palm tree, and aside from his plow's steel tip and cooking utensils consumes almost no nonreplenishable resources. Compare him with the New York executive with his private jet, air-conditioned mansion, and all the rest.

The affluent New Yorker may consume 25,000 or 50,000 times as much energy as a Javanese peasant.

The Christian Science Monitor (March 7, 1974)

. . . and our Posterity . . .

As always, men and women will lash out against the obvious threats to their health and well-being. They will attack nuclear power plants and oil refineries, paper mills and automobile factories, tanneries and steel mills. At the same time, unfortunately, very few will ask questions about their own demand for electrical energy, for fuel, for paper, for automobiles, shoes and steel products. Very few will question the damage they are causing as part of a consumption-oriented society.

> EDMUND M. MUSKIE, U.S. Senator from Maine, in a speech at Chicago (January 1970)

If you truly amend your ways and your doings,
if you truly execute justice one with another,
if you do not oppress the alien,
the fatherless or the widow,
or shed innocent blood in this place,
and if you do not go after other gods to your own hurt,
then I will let you dwell in this place,
in the land that I gave of old to your fathers for ever.

> JEREMIAH 7:5-7

Tribe follows tribe, and nation follows nation, like the waves of the sea. It is the order of nature, and regret is useless. Your time of decay may be distant—but it will surely come, for even the White Man whose God walked and talked with him as friend with friend, can not be exempt from the common destiny. We may be brothers after all. We will see.

> SEALTH (SEATTLE), Chief of the Duwamish, in an address to Isaac Stevens, Governor of Washington Territory (1855)

In God We Trust.

> Motto on the dollar bill

Only a few years ago British author-statesman C. P. Snow warned Americans it might not be long before they began to view global famine on their living-room TV set.

The cruel irony, . . . which Lord Snow did not forecast, is that it is beginning to be appreciated that the energy consumed by that TV set, if converted into fertilizer and food, might save the lives of those seen starving on the screen.

Can Americans afford affluence at such a high human price?

> *The Christian Science Monitor* (March 7, 1974)

Man has an inherent capacity to react against his own extremism. St. Francis of Assisi wed his Lady Poverty just as the commercialism of the high Middle Ages

enforced its grip on the Italian cities. Quaker protests
became potent in the licentious Britain of the Stuart
Restoration. Wesley preached the Gospel to a gin-
soaked proletariat. Indeed, the origins of all the great
world religions in the millenia before the birth of Christ
appear to have lain in a planetary revulsion against the
violence and greed of the early river civilizations.

After hundreds of years of devastating civil war in
China, Confucius preached the social virtues of toler-
ance, temperance and obedience. The Hindu mystics
and the Lord Buddha dismissed as illusion the violent
Indian world of warriors and feuding princes. After the
defeats and tribal strife of the Dorian invasions, the
Greeks came to believe that shrieking furies struck
down the over-mighty man. In place of pride and force,
they looked to reason and restraint as the marks of
virtue. Amid the rise and fall of Middle Eastern empires, the Jewish prophets heard God speak in a "still,
small voice" asking obedience, not holocausts of victims. And it was in the "high and palmy state" of
triumphant Roman imperialism that Christ conse-
crated all sacrifice, all humility, all reconciliation by
His own Death.

In every case, a surfeit of violence, arrogance and
rapacity brought on the renewed hunger for spiritual
vision. Is it not possible, after 400 years of the post-
Renaissance outburst of driving, world-changing
energies—the most superb and destructive adventure

in human history—that once again the spirit of man
may feel the uneasiness of surfeit and be ready to swing
the pendulum of experience and vital intelligence back
from the ways of conquest to the ways of patience and
restraint? We do not know. But the signs of change
cannot be dismissed by modern man, least of all by
Christians whose master is Lord of the whole earth, of
all living things, and Whose will it is that they should
be preserved in love and peace.

> BARBARA WARD, in *A New Creation?: Reflections
> on the Environmental Issue* (1973), pp. 68–69

Choose life,
that you and your descendants may live.

DEUTERONOMY 30:19

According to his promise
we wait for new heavens
and a new earth
in which righteousness dwells.

2 PETER 3:13

As evangelical Christians committed to the Lord Jesus
Christ and the full authority of the Word of God, we
affirm that God lays total claim upon the lives of his

people. We cannot, therefore, separate our lives in Christ from the situation in which God has placed us in the United States and the world.

We confess that we have not acknowledged the complete claims of God on our lives.

We acknowledge that God requires love. But we have not demonstrated the love of God to those suffering social abuses.

We acknowledge that God requires justice. But we have not proclaimed or demonstrated his justice to an unjust American society. Although the Lord calls us to defend the social and economic rights of the poor and the oppressed, we have mostly remained silent. We deplore the historic involvement of the church in America with racism and the conspicuous responsibility of the evangelical community for perpetuating the personal attitudes and institutional structures that have divided the body of Christ along color lines. Further, we have failed to condemn the exploitation of racism at home and abroad by our economic system.

We affirm that God abounds in mercy and that he forgives all who repent and turn from their sins. So we call our fellow evangelical Christians to demonstrate repentance in a Christian discipleship that confronts that social and political injustice of our nation.

We must attack the materialism of our culture and the maldistribution of the nation's wealth and services. We recognize that as a nation we play a crucial role in the imbalance and injustice of international trade and development. Before God and a billion hungry neighbors, we must rethink our values regarding our present standard of living and promote more just acquisition and distribution of the world's resources.

We acknowledge our Christian responsibilities of citizenship. Therefore, we must challenge the misplaced trust of the nation in economic and military might—a proud trust that promotes a national pathology of war and violence which victimizes our neighbors at home and abroad. We must resist the temptation to make the nation and its institutions objects of near-religious loyalty.

We acknowledge that we have encouraged men to prideful domination and women to irresponsible passivity. So we call both men and women to mutual submission and active discipleship.

We proclaim no new gospel, but the Gospel of our Lord Jesus Christ who, through the power of the Holy Spirit, frees people from sin so that they might praise God through works of righteousness.

By this declaration, we endorse no political ideology or party, but call our nation's leaders and people to that righteousness which exalts a nation.

We make this declaration in the biblical hope that Christ is coming to consummate the Kingdom and we accept his claim on our total discipleship till He comes.

> *A Declaration of Evangelical Social Concern*, originally signed by 53 evangelical leaders in Chicago, Illinois (November 1973)

It is easy to scoff at this vision of our humanity, our oneness, our common task as fellow passengers on a small planet. The great and powerful of this earth, including those of America and Europe, can easily sniff cynically and return to their game of power politics, national jealousies, mountains of armaments, millions of graves of men mourned by widows and orphans, ravaged oceans, unverdant plains, and hungry homeless people who despair of the good life. But somehow I believe there is enough good will in our country and in the world to expect millions of people to declare all of this powerful posturing of corrupt politicians to be arrant nonsense in one world, to say that we do want all men and women to be brothers and sisters, that we do believe in justice and peace, and that we think homes, fields of grain, schools, and medicine are better than guns, tanks, submarines, ABMs and MIRVs. The trouble is that the millions of little people, the ones who really man Spaceship Earth, the ones who really work and suffer and die while the politicians posture and play, these little ones have never been given a chance to declare themselves. And this is wrong, globally wrong.

Having traveled across the face of our beautiful planet, having traversed all its oceans and its continents, having shared deep human hopes with my brothers and sisters of every nationality, religion, color, and race, having broken bread and found loving friendship and brotherhood everywhere on earth, I am prepared this day to declare myself a citizen of the world, and to invite everyone everywhere to embrace this vision of our interdependent world, our common humanity, our noblest hopes and our common quest for justice in our times and, ultimately, for peace on earth, now, and in the next millennium.

THEODORE M. HESBURGH, in *The Humane Imperative* (1974), pp. 114–15

Then I saw a new heaven and a new earth;
for the first heaven and the first earth
had passed away, and the sea was no more.
And I saw the holy city, new Jerusalem,
coming down out of heaven from God,
prepared as a bride adorned for her husband;
and I heard a great voice from the throne saying,
"Behold, the dwelling of God is with men.
He will dwell with them,
and they shall be his people,
and God himself will be with them;
he will wipe away every tear from their eyes,
and death shall be no more,
neither shall there be mourning
nor crying nor pain any more,
for the former things have passed away."

And he who sat upon the throne said,
"Behold, I make all things new."

REVELATION 21:1–5

. . . with liberty and justice for all.
Pledge to the Flag

If we are going to bequeath a new world to "our posterity," we must have a change of heart, a conversion which will lead to a society "with liberty and justice for all." THE SHAKERTOWN PLEDGE GROUP invites Americans to make the following pledge as we approach our third century:

Recognizing that the earth and the fulness thereof is a gift from our gracious God, and that we are called to cherish, nurture, and provide loving stewardship for the earth's resources,

And recognizing that life itself is a gift, and a call to responsibility, joy, and celebration,

I make the following declarations:

1. I declare myself to be a world citizen.
2. I commit myself to lead an ecologically sound life.
3. I commit myself to lead a life of creative simplicity and to share my personal wealth with the world's poor.
4. I commit myself to join with others in reshaping institutions in order to bring about a more just global society in which each person has full access to the needed resources for their physical, emotional, intellectual, and spiritual growth.

5. I commit myself to occupational accountability, and in so doing I will seek to avoid the creation of products which cause harm to others.
6. I affirm the gift of my body, and commit myself to its proper nourishment and physical well-being.
7. I commit myself to examine continually my relations with others, and to attempt to relate honestly, morally, and lovingly to those around me.
8. I commit myself to personal renewal through prayer, meditation, and study.
9. I commit myself to responsible participation in a community of faith.

For more information on the pledge and the group, write THE SHAKERTOWN PLEDGE GROUP, 4719 Cedar Avenue, Philadelphia, Pennsylvania 19143.

Index of Sources and Groups

(Groups indicated by SMALL CAPITAL LETTERS*)*

Index of Scriptural Quotations

OLD TESTAMENT

NEW TESTAMENT

For readers of *The Patriot's Bible* . . .

the radical bible

Adapted by John Eagleson and Philip Scharper

In its fourth printing

"*The Radical Bible* claws at the reader's conscience and mind in just the way God's Word has always been meant to—but the Bible alone for most of us no longer has this effect, since familiarity has blunted the point and repetition dulled the edge of this Sword of the Spirit. Scripture passages are blended with statistics, vignettes, and statements from the modern world of major Christian churches and contemporary international leaders and organizations.

"*The Radical Bible* will easily fit into your denim or dress shirt pocket, or purse, and I would urge that you put one there for reading at odd moments of your day-to-day life. It might just get some of us off dead-center! A challenging gift for anyone."

—*Provident Book Finder*

"Most effective medium for the message I've seen."
—Colman Barry, O.S.B., Chairman, Dept. of Religious Studies, Catholic University of America

ISBN 0-88344-4259
ISBN 0-88344-4267

Cloth $3.95
Paper $1.95

At your local bookstore or order directly from
Orbis Books, Maryknoll, New York 10545